MW00513446

Let's Talk Story

Wisdom is in the Ordinary
if You Know How to Look

Arnie Weimerskirch
&
John Fechter

ISBN: 978-1-09834-335-4

Let's Talk Story

<u>Preface – the view from John's chair</u>

A favorite place growing up and now is Glacier National Park in Montana. Aside from the natural beauty, it is a place of learning and wisdom. Especially so when tribal members from the adjoining Blackfeet Indian Reservation joined us around evening campfires to share their culture, their view of the world and the meaning of the park. And when reading their collected stories of passed down lore now available in print.

A truly wonderful part of their culture is respect for their elders and high value placed on nurturing and teaching Blackfeet culture to the children. A highlight method for doing that is storytelling.

In American culture, prescriptive laws and prescriptive standards are generally the rule. Do this. Don't do that. But the Blackfeet approach has an added dimension – to communicate values and manners and rules and morals and expectations by stories. For example, instead of reprimanding or lecturing children about the prescriptive right or wrong of some behavior, they used stories -- often called Old Man stories -- to illustrate lessons learned by people and animals as they encountered the good and bad in the world.

Hearing those stories gave me a lifetime perspective to pay attention – not just to what was happening in front of my own eyes. Not just the facts of what was happening, but the lessons I could take away by also understanding WHY and HOW, not just WHAT.

And the beauty of this approach meant that the important lessons the world presented to me had personality and reality that are absent from a clinical view. Einstein's $e=mc^2$ is a clinically accurate formula but its impact on my life is best illustrated in a story.

Arnie and I have worked together at the same company, and then for different companies, and with multiple technical groups. It has been a pleasure because we've shared decades of interesting things that passed our way. We noticed WHAT we were seeing. And when we talked about the particulars with each other we also saw the wisdom of the HOW and the WHY. From those many conversations we took away lessons that we kept in our quiver for future use.

This book is a collection of some funny, serious, important, and trivial things that the world presented to us. And in the fashion of the Blackfeet tales describing wisdom, we want to Talk Story – to share them with you, for four reasons:

1) They describe some interesting events,

2) The wisdom within the events can apply to your world, and

3) The approach will optimize your filter so that more and more often you will see not just what is happening but also see the wisdom and lessons within, and

4) Our biggest hope is that we can pass along that skill to help you by using our stories or use this approach to find one in your own life experience that illustrates by story what you want to share with your team, your family, your colleagues.

Preface – the view from Arnie's chair

I have often wondered why it took me so long to learn some of life's most basic lessons. Lessons like active listening, simplifying daily life, accepting responsibility, succeeding in an organization and many more. I didn't learn these lessons from textbooks. The textbooks used in formal education teach a basic set of skills that can be used to do productive work. They teach theories that the student can apply to their own situation. They may teach one how to earn a living, but they don't teach one how to succeed in life.

To be successful in life, one needs to be "street savvy." One needs to learn how and when to apply the things taught by formal education. We learn this by experience through the school of "hard knocks." It is often said that experience is the best teacher, but tuition can be expensive.

My co-author, John, and I have worked together for over thirty years. Our careers have followed parallel paths. We have been fortunate to travel to many places and have had many unique experiences in our lifetime. We have been exposed to variety of cultures which forced us to understand, communicate with, and cooperate with many different ways of thinking. In the span of our careers, we have seen dramatic advances in technology, the advent of globalization, and an increasingly competitive environment. These forces have driven a change in management philosophy from "If it ain't broke, don't fix it" to a compelling need for breakthrough thinking and continual improvement. Yet, the lessons we learned have proved to be timeless. Human cultural behavior changes only on a glacial, evolutionary basis.

Frequently, as we worked together, John and I would reflect on our experiences and wonder if there was a way that we could help people learn life's lessons in a shorter time span than we had. Could we reverse the process used by formal education? Could we describe our experiences from a practical point of view and then extract a theory (lessons learned) that other people could apply to their own circumstances? Could we capture our life's experiences between the two covers of a book in a way that would permit people to go to the school of "hard knocks" without paying the high price of tuition over many years?

We decided that the best way to do that is through a four-step process:

1) Tell our stories exactly as we lived and experienced them.

2) Describe how we went about learning from that experience

3) Extrapolate lessons learned for the benefit of the reader.

4) Explain how readers can apply the lesson learned to their own life.

We want to take this opportunity to share these stories and lessons with you. Some of our stories apply to an organizational environment. Others are simply stories from everyday life. Each story taught us a lesson that enabled us to lead a more successful life. We think these lessons might be helpful to you too.

ABOUT THIS BOOK

This is not an ordinary book. It is an unusual book. It consists of many stories telling of our life experiences and the lessons we learned from them.

You do not have to read the book from start to finish. There is no chronological order to the book and there is no relationship among the stories. We have included a detailed Table of Contents, summarizing the stories and their lesson. You can browse the Table of Contents and pick and choose the articles you want to read. You can start anywhere in the book with whatever story seems interesting to you. That will make for efficient reading.

All of the stories in this book are real with real people, real places and real experiences. In order to comply with privacy laws, we do not use names in the book even when we mentioned them in a positive way. None of our stories are fictional.

We are not management experts. We have no profound leadership theories to profess. We are simply two executives who each have worked in industry or academia for over 40 years and gained real life experiences. Our experiences happened at a point in time, but the stories and their meaning are timeless. As we lived these experiences and learned these lessons, we came to recognize the underlying principle involved, not just the specifics of the task at hand. We baked these principles into our repertoire to influence all other jobs we did. They became an integral part of our skill set. By sharing these stories, we hope to enable you to see not only the task at hand, but to also see the lifelong lessons so you can add to your own repertoire for all your future endeavors.

When leading teams – from project level teams to company-wide functions – storytelling is a highly effective tool to convey intent, importance, why, and what the future will look like. People need specifics but the story is what moves them. We hope our stories help you by being useful examples in their own right, or by helping you convey your message with your own story.

A common thread in this book is the concept that the results you get are caused by the actions you take. If actions are taken at random, the result will be chaos. If actions are carried out in an orderly manner, the results will be good. The lessons we learned teach us that if we take the right actions, we will get the results we desire.

ABOUT THE AUTHORS

Arnold Weimerskirch is a retired Vice President of
Quality for Honeywell, Inc. and former chairman of
the panel of judges for the Malcolm Baldrige
National Quality Award. He is co-author of *Total
Quality Management - Strategies and Techniques
Proven at Today's Most Successful Companies.* He
holds BS and MS engineering degrees from the
University of Minnesota. He lives with his wife,
Anne, in Wayzata, Minnesota.

John Fechter is a retired senior executive --
Honeywell, Inc., Honeywell Bull, and KeyCorp, and
is a Medtronic Lean Sigma Master Black Belt. He
has been an adjunct professor for over 25 years at
the University of St. Thomas in St. Paul, Minnesota,
and program director for its M.S. in Technology
Management degree. His best job ever was as a
mountaintop fire lookout for the U.S. Forest Service
in Montana. He holds BS and MS degrees from
Montana State University and a PhD in Psychology
(ergonomics specialty) from the University of South
Dakota. He and his wife, Judy, live in Blaine,
Minnesota.

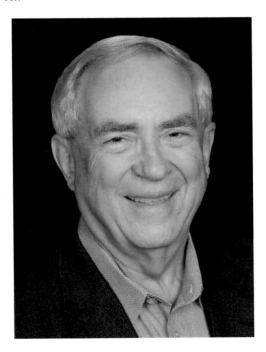

Table of Contents

Expanded Table of Contents, Story, Theme, Lessons Learned

01 Personal Well Being

📖 Positive thinking   Page 60

- o **Story:** A learning experience
- o **Theme:** A workshop on positive thinking demonstrates the importance of having a high regard for yourself and not being unduly influenced by other people's criticism.
- o **Lessons Learned:** Positive thinking is a powerful attribute. People should have a high regard for themselves. They should strive to achieve everything they can and then be comfortable with themselves.

📖 What do you do after you don't have a business card?   Page 64

- o **Story:** Contemplating retirement
- o **Theme:** In contemplating retirement, I discover that the most important factor is not what to do with my time, but rather how to replace the socialization that work provides.
- o **Lessons Learned:** There are two basic principles of retirement:
    - o Get to know yourself
    - o Socialization is the most important consideration in retirement

02 Following the Golden Rule

- o **Story:** A bank teller's integrity and compassion helped an elderly man discover the collection-value of his coins so he could pay for his wife's surgery.
- o **Theme:** He waited patiently for the next teller. She emptied his bag and counted it out—something around $300. She noticed many were still shiny though with long-ago dates on them. She called the coin collection dealer across the street to come and appraise. Its value was far, far above the $300 cash value. He made an offer, which was accepted with smiles and a hearty "Thank You."
- o **Lessons Learned:** The teller was guided by her values and compassion to do the right thing. Her small, extra action produced results far beyond a basic banking transaction. Values, rather than prescriptive rules and regulations, show us a bright standard through which we can look at our immediate circumstances and know the right thing to do.

📖 **Why didn't you pound the counter?** Page 89

- o **Story:** KLM gate agents in Amsterdam confront a room full of passengers from two, full 747s trying to get seats aboard a single 747.
- o **Theme:** Amsterdam departure gate. Pandemonium as people from a returned flight and ours – both 747s – demand a seat. Impossible. Others yelled, pounded fists. Handing out the last two boarding passes, the agent said to me "Don't say anything. Here are your boarding passes. Get on board". She had bumped us to First Class for my courtesy -- I had treated her as a human being, not a servant.
- o **Lessons Learned:** Friendliness and kindness are free. It doesn't cost anything to be pleasant, but it makes all the difference in the world. No matter their station in life, all people deserve respect and kindness. You are not better than them; they are not better than you.

03 Simplifying daily life

📖 Angry ranchers in the ranger's office
Page 99

- **Story:** Ranchers who "had the Ranger's permission" to graze cattle in the national forest exceeded the number allowed. Past permissions were neither dated nor documented.
- **Theme:** Handshake agreements don't survive when the parties who shook hands way back when have left the scene. Put it in writing before they depart.
- **Lessons Learned:** Put it in writing. Others who come after you need to know what you did, what you said, and what you agreed to. As we listened to the arguing, we noted as a life lesson, "Always put a name and **date on every version of every document.**"

📖 Super-efficient gastronomical delight
Page 105

- **Story:** Efficiently optimize the start of the day. Co-equal deliverables timed to be ready simultaneously -- a complicated breakfast and the morning newspapers.
- **Theme:** What makes a perfect start of the day? Reading the New York Times and the StarTribune while eating a piping hot, spicy breakfast! An everyday example illustrates how tools of production efficiency can also optimize daily, personal tasks.
- **Lessons Learned:** These tools work at work and at home. When "in the process", step back and observe. Take time to appreciate what is happening and then you can have the perspective to work "on the process."

📖 **Think of your work as a process**
Page 112

- o **Story:** The general's story
- o **Theme:** A four-star general defines his daily routine as a process and uses processes throughout his organization.
- o **Lessons Learned:** All work can be defined as a process. Processes detail the methods by which work is performed. Processes should be continually improved and made more efficient.

04 Communicating Effectively

📖 **Active listening** Page 123
- ○ **Story:** Getting it right
- ○ **Theme:** I learn the art of active listening and how to empathize with people.
- ○ **Lessons Learned:** Organizations and individuals should learn and practice the art of ACTIVE LISTENING. It makes communications more effective and enables deeper understanding of the other person's viewpoints and objectives.

📖 **Ask more questions** Page 127
- ○ **Story:** I erroneously applied his answer to a question I inferred but hadn't actually asked.
- ○ **Theme:** "We moving to Boston?" Red laughed and answered, "I'm not moving to Boston!" We both laughed." What he said was, "I'm not moving to Boston." I inferred that headquarters staff were not moving to Boston. Later, we moved headquarters to Boston. Red stayed in Minnesota.
- ○ **Lessons Learned:** *1.* People often hear first what they want to hear. *2.* Murphy's Law: anything that can go wrong, will go wrong. Perhaps Murphy's cousin used another saying, "Whatever can be misunderstood will be misunderstood." *3.* As the saying goes, if you assume but don't say the assumptions out loud, you risk making an ASS out of U and ME. *4.* Verify that you got it right, before you take action.

📖 Don't surprise me in front of my boss
Page 134

- Story: We had been so enthusiastic to analyze the customer satisfaction results and prepare our presentation that we had not included time to brief executives-- about their processes and customer satisfaction -- in advance of the company-wide operations meeting.

- Theme: A much delayed customer satisfaction survey put the spotlight on several internal processes, exposing gaps needing attention and action. But during the presentation, senior management harshly commented to various process owners who -- like everyone else -- had only just now seen the data, asking why they hadn't fixed these just-uncovered problems.

- Lessons Learned: My lifelong lesson: <u>Don't Surprise Me in Front of My Boss.</u> If you learn something important that is beyond your own responsibilities, share the information in a timely manner with others who own the process. Those people are key stakeholders and the odds that they will help improve things are much increased the sooner they hear that their corrective action is needed.

📖 Everyday outstanding flight attendant
Page 139

- Story: Normal, everyday tasks involving other people are opportunities in disguise.

- Theme: Often-repeated interactions with clients/customers can become tedious and boring, and consequently done in a pro forma, bland, and passive way. Or, the same tasks, done with polish and personality, can have those clients/customers charmed and listening closely. Which result happens is up to you.

- Lessons Learned: Too much of our day-to-day social interaction is done by habit and everyday communications become background noise. Communicate, don't just say the words in the script. Done well, they will STOP, LOOK, and LISTEN. And smile.

📖 OK, but will it hurt   Page 144

- **Story:** A caring physician, a doting mother, and a trusting little boy puzzled and fearful -- why did they need to "cut off his feet"?
- **Theme:** "We need to cut off your feet." Does that sentence give you pause? He was about 3-4 years old. They saw that he'd outgrown his pajamas and they made him stoop as he walked. He thought they were going to cut off his feet to make him shorter.
- **Lessons Learned:** People perceive things through the filter of their own beliefs, emotions, and knowledge. Even though you are transmitting properly doesn't mean that the other person will receive the message you intended to send. Be aware of how other people are receiving your message. Is their body language at odds with what you expected? An easy technique is to ask them to tell you what they heard from you -- in their own words.

📖 Rank has its privileges – or not
Page 150

- o **Story:** An expert in Australia
- o **Theme:** During a trip to Australia, when I was Chairman of the Baldrige Judges Panel, I was assumed to have knowledge just because of my position. People asked me questions about which I had no knowledge.
- o **Lessons Learned:** People assume competence based on a person's status whether that competence is real or not. This tendency inhibits communications and fails to take advantage of all the knowledge present. Synergy is a very important concept. In any group meeting, every individual has a piece of the information that is valuable to achieve the group's objective.

05 Accepting Responsibility

📖 Big or small, do it right or not at all
Page 157

- **Story:** "I remembered the job interview when I said for quality, 'Do it right, or not at all.' And because I wasn't sure I could do it right, I didn't do it at all."

- **Theme:** This was her first job. She understood the feedback and that she should take action to enable her to do it right the first time. As time went by, when we discussed similar assignments and projects she needed to do, she would have a quick smile and a comment, "Do it right. And that's all."

- **Lessons Learned:** When receiving an assignment, say it back in your own words. That's measuring twice to confirm what you're being asked to do. Empower people: empowered means that a person has the means to deliver what their customer or client expects from them. Objectively critique performance – the processes currently in use - - without criticizing or blaming the person.

- o **Story:** Noticing smoke wafting above a dry forest, it became "my" job to stop it from becoming a forest fire.
- o **Theme:** Last night's dry lightning started a tree to smolder. Because I noticed it, it became "my" job to stop it from becoming a forest fire. My behavior and personal motivation were noted by Forest Service personnel charged with forest management and fire suppression. They used my initiative as an interview and hired me.
- o **Lessons Learned:** If you see something that needs attention, action, or help – do something if it is within your power to make it happen. Live your values. People who do the right thing and jump in when circumstances call for it – whether it's been assigned to them or not – move to the "short list" of people you want on your team.

- o **Story:** A hard trip
- o **Theme:** It required persistence for me and my colleague to make a difficult business trip. It taught us a valuable lifetime lesson.
- o **Lessons Learned:** Sometimes it takes persistence to make the right things happen. Life is like that too. It is not always easy. Many studies show that persistence is the most critical element of success.

📖 **When management tells you to do the wrong thing**   Page 174

o **Story:** Frustrated with my bank
o **Theme:** My bank had rules and regulations that seemed to be unreasonable and were a great inconvenience to me. Another organization applied their rules with judgement with a much better outcome.
o **Lessons Learned:** Organizations should create a culture that encourages employees to use judgment in their everyday work. Employees should be motivated to be well informed about their organization's rules and procedures and to question them when they appear to be unreasonable. Customer focus should be the number one priority.

06 Gaining Knowledge

📖 **Kids in the class!**   Page 181

o **Story:** I love teaching if there are *kids* in the class!

o **Theme:** While making a short, promotional video about the Master of Science in Technology Management program at the University of St. Thomas, I was asked, "Why do you teach?" My answer: Because my graduate students are kids. Kids ask WHY? WHAT IF? COULD WE...? Kids are eager to see what new things can help. "Kids" want to learn because they want to do things they don't yet know how to do.

o **Lessons Learned:** Curiosity is almost a life force. Encourage it and reward it. Adult engineers are kids when they have a chance to learn hard-earned lessons from the experience of others and then try new things that go beyond established principles.

📖 Knowledge earns respect   Page 186

- ○ **Story:** Getting the right information
- ○ **Theme:** I became frustrated with my pest control company when I had a problem with pocket gophers. Two employees did not give me satisfactory answers about why they could not solve my problem. A third employee had more knowledge and gave me a satisfactory answer.

- ○ **Lessons Learned:** Every employee, in the course to their everyday job, comes in contact with people -- usually customers -- who are looking for information and guidance. An answer of "I don't know" means "I don't care." Employees should always be trying to expand their knowledge of their job and environment so that they can respond. This is largely a matter of attitude. The result is that they will receive positive feedback and their job will be more rewarding.

07 Understanding Human Nature

📖 **I can't read cursive**   Page 191
o **Story:** Upon receiving my notes on their draft report, students asked for help: "We need you to go through all of your handwritten comments. We don't read cursive."
o **Theme:**
- "You got the job, why are you still home?"
- "How did I know I got the job?"
- "I left a handwritten note on your door."
- "I saw the note, but I can't read cursive handwriting."

o **Lessons Learned:** I cannot assume that the things I've learned in my culture and experiences I've had are universally known and understood. Our perspective and filters are separated from one another by geography, by the eras I have lived in versus the eras of others, by the contrast of village life, metropolitan life, or country life...

📖 **Who pays the price?**   Page 196
o **Story:** International Ergonomics Association 1979 -- first meeting behind the Communist "iron curtain"
o **Theme:** Asked about workplace safety, injuries, accidents, deaths -- Communist Party tour guide replied "...Polish workers – especially in mining -- were devoting their lives to bringing Poland back to being a great culture and a strong economy... Deaths and injuries are considered 'casualties of war' Once victorious ... and once again powerful, then Poland could invest time to improve worker safety." Did workers know they were in an economic "war", and they were considered expendable? Was the economic situation truly so dire that expenses for better training and safety were unaffordable?

- o **Lessons Learned:** Sometimes, our assumptions about shared truths may be ignored by others who see a larger game at play. Mission, vision, values, and goals said aloud become reference points. With them, we can expose gaps that must be closed in order to change those mission, vision, values, goal statements facts rather than just aspirations. In a transparent organization, motives are clear because there are no hidden missions, no hidden visions, no hidden values, and no hidden goals.

Understanding global cultures
Page 205

- o **Story:** Around the world
- o **Theme:** As I traveled worldwide, I encountered many different cultures. I learned the importance of understanding those cultures and accepting the people who come from different cultural backgrounds.
- o **Lessons Learned:** There is more to global communications that just language. Culture is important. Take time to dig deeper than the language barrier. Get to know the customs and values of people from other countries. Get to know how they think and why they act the way they do.

I thought you spoke English
Page 209

- **Story:** Your English accent is very difficult to understand
- **Theme:** French was her natural language. She had honed her spoken English while living in Kenya. Kenya-accented English is such a strong accent as to be nearly unrecognized by people outside of Kenya. She could hardly decipher our American-accented English.
- **Lessons Learned:** Same as *"I can't read cursive"* article: I cannot assume that the things I've learned in my culture and that the experiences I've had are universally known and understood. Our perspective and filters are separated from one another by geography, by the eras I have lived in versus the eras of others, by the contrast of village life, metropolitan life, or country life...

08 Thinking Outside the Box

- o **Story:** Listeners jumped to conclusions -- startled and offended by what they heard -- until they realized it wasn't what they heard.

- o **Theme:** A business dinner with senior executives and their spouses. Multiple strangers. A traveler's story shared with all, upsetting people during its telling. After their upset disappeared, they forced me to tell the story to others while those "previously upset" people watched new listeners go through the same incredulous discomfort and then break out in laughter at the surprise ending.

- o **Lessons Learned:** Listeners fill in the blanks but don't interrupt to verify with the speaker. The story was funny, and its humor was a useful icebreaker to encourage people to listen and ask questions if something they heard wasn't clear. Especially helpful when starting new projects with people speaking other languages and living in other cultures.

09 Working in an organization

📖 Customer delight   Page 268
- o **Story:** Delight 'em
- o **Theme:** Honeywell's CEO's license plate read "Delight 'em". Delighting customers is a science that can be put into practice.
- o **Lessons Learned:** Customer satisfaction has several dimensions. Relationships and brand recognition are equally as important as the price and the product or service offered. Customers are loyal when their expectations are exceeded.

📖 Minnesota nice misunderstood   Page 273
- o **Story:** Teamwork with a supplier was thwarted when they changed the rules mid-stream.
- o **Theme:** Past dealings with engineers, procurement, and production personnel had shown a "Minnesota Nice" face when working issues with this supplier. An engineering team flew to the supplier's site to resolve quality issues together on the production floor. Entry was halted unless we signed non-disclosure forms -- though we'd agreed beforehand they wouldn't be required. We turned around and flew home.
- o **Lessons Learned:** Be nice, trust your suppliers. But facts are facts and if the suppliers change terms unilaterally or fail to live up to their agreements, say a "nice" goodbye and find another course of action.

📖 Promotion to action   Page 277

- o **Story:** People are promoted to increase the leverage of their actions. TMII interferes with doing that well.
- o **Theme:** *Too Much Irrelevant Information* makes it hard to separate the information you need from a stream of data filled with irrelevant information.
- o **Lessons Learned:** To filter out distracting or useless information, I need to ask,
  "What do I need to know?"
    - to manage a process,
    - to find defects,
    - to minimize cycle time, etc.

📖 Servant leadership   Page 288

- o **Story:** Shading the truth
- o **Theme:** A Production Manager gets my department into trouble by not telling the truth. I learned a lesson about "hands-on" management.
- o **Lessons Learned:** A great deal of information is lost as communications travel up and down the chain of command. People are afraid that they will be blamed for problems and will be reprimanded. As a result, they often bend the truth. The concept of servant leadership puts management in the position of solving problems rather than punishing employees.

📖 Value creation   Page 292
- o **Story:** Defining world-class
- o **Theme:** I create a vision of world-class performance and a VALUE CREATION MODEL which leads Honeywell to superior business success.
- o **Lessons Learned:** Organizations exist to create value for all of their stakeholders. There is a complementary relationship among stakeholders – the more value the organization creates for one stakeholder the more value it creates for all stakeholders. Organizations that create outstanding stakeholder value share a common set of world-class characteristics.

📖 You actually read those memos?   Page 298
- o **Story:** Letters, memos, e-mails without specific requests for action are ignored or forgotten.
- o **Theme:** Recipients of weekly management report were free to read the updates, but it was their own decision to take any particular action. Wasted time and uncertain expectations were common.

- o A new standard was created:
    1. all communications must have an ACTION element (FYI was OK; only TO recipients could be given an action),
    2. a SUMMARY to give context, and
    3. a BACKGROUND if you wanted to include it.
- o **Lessons Learned:** Fewer memos were needed, and fewer people received them. The sender had the responsibility to request ACTION and had to be specific. The culture changed to communicating results or issues with accompanying recommendations or requests, and people expected to see Who was supposed to do What and by When.

📖 You just shut down production   Page 304

- o **Story:** No exceptions after 31 December. I need your cost center number; you stopped production and we can't ship.

- o **Theme:** No one took ownership of when a "reasonable period of time" had passed and old-company-name parts would cease to be used. I called a meeting of executives who owned various processes. All agreed on a cease-using date, but we neglected to confirm Who will do What by When actions -- before we closed the meeting.

- o **Lessons Learned:** Knowing what the end point looks like is not enough. The many steps to reach that end point -- using only the new company's name on all parts and publications -- were not described and that lack of action crashed into the 31 December limit.

- o The plan must include not only the end point, but also a plan noting what resources are needed, and who will do what by when.

10 Results, not hopes

📖 Customer satisfaction   Page 313

o **Story:** Flying to Europe
o **Theme:** A customer satisfaction survey about a trip to Europe failed to collect the most important information.
o **Lessons Learned:** What you measure is what you manage. The most fundamental reason to collect data and measure something is to improve. It is important to get information not just data. Setting numerical goals can be detrimental if employees don't understand the purpose of the measurement.

📖 I got flamed   Page 317

o **Story:** If people thought nothing was changing though changes were needed, making a commotion may look like progress. It's not.
o **Theme:** We need to improve! All agreed. Dozens of projects were started, lots of meetings held, lots of talking -- but people did not know what FINISHED looked like. So, I asked each project to define what success looked like and cancelled projects if they couldn't define it. I got flamed; many believed that activity without change was still progress.
o **Lessons Learned:** Without a clear picture of what the end point looks like, projects flounder, consume time, funds, and effort, but in the end many projects were all for naught. Be specific -- to achieve a measurable goal by this date.

📖 **Eureka -- puzzle solved**   Page 322

- ○ **Story:** "Despite the fact that customer needs can become very numerous, each requires a means of measurement, a goal, a product, and a process design." Dr. Joe Juran.
- ○ **Theme:** For every expected result -- big and little results -- you need a process to deliver the result. For every process you need data showing how it is working. If you cannot articulate the results expected you cannot create the right process and cannot measure whether or not everything is working properly.
- ○ **Lessons Learned:** No exceptions. The *Expected Results Matrix* must include every goal, wish, hope, expectation, or similar. And for each item in the matrix, describe the Process of how that goal will happen. And for every process and every step, articulate the measures needed be sure everything is working correctly.

📖 Rich and famous   Page 329

- **Story:** Simply describing a brighter future won't make it happen. Say aloud what you need ME to do to help make it happen.
- **Theme:** Lofty statements about a better tomorrow have no value if I cannot see a way to make those lofty statements become reality. It's not a magic act -- show me what needs doing and what I need to do. How will I know we're there?
- **Lessons Learned:** State the goals, *measure ARE WE THERE YET?* If not yet, find gaps. Prioritize which gaps are most important. Develop a plan to close gaps. Then, act. *START, STOP, KEEP.* Without action, the status quo repeats endlessly.

📖 Use data to make decisions   Page 337

- **Story:** Touring Japan
- **Theme:** On one of my trips to Japan, I was impressed with how they use data in everyday life to make decisions based on fact.
- **Lessons Learned:** It is important to use data (evidence) to make decisions. This is known as evidenced based management. Evidenced based management is a matter of determining the desired result and then identifying the data (evidence) that needs to be collected to determine the facts. By analyzing this data, actions can be taken to achieve the desired result.

What's the secret formula?   Page 340

- o **Story:** Step back. Watch the process from a distance. It will tell you how to make it better.
- o **Theme:** Nothing happens by chance. Sometimes we want coffee, but the process gives us tea. Why? Every process is a collection of cause and effect pieces. If you know how to look, it will tell you what to change so you always get coffee.
- o **Lessons Learned:** Three secrets:
  - Cause & effect, does the cost of improvement show a good Return on Investment for making the changes?
  - Very specifically -- what needs to START that isn't happening now, what needs to STOP, and what is just fine and needs to KEEP being part of the process.
  - And can you objectively measure if, and how well, the changes worked?

Chapter 01
Personal Well Being

Deer march

THE STORY

I'm deep in sleep.
3am.

Technology is always awake.

> **Nature can teach us if we patiently watch**

MOTION DETECTED by the exterior floodlights facing the wetlands! Lights quickly change from off to full-on and the back yard and wetlands are now bright as a theater stage.

I'm fully awake! Up goes the bedroom shade so I can see why the lights turned on.

I watch the scene. It is a small herd of deer in very late fall. During the summer they mostly roam independently. But with the coming of cold weather and fall colors, the deer gather into a small herd of 7-9, staying together through the fall and winter.

It is a delight to see them form the annual herd; it signals the coming of fall. Each evening, when daylight changes to alpenglow -- just before sunset -- the yearlings frolic and the adults watch, munching on whatever is still green.

But this morning at 3am it is late fall, the season that brings longer and colder nights.

The deer are unaffected by the motion-detecting floodlights coming on at 3am. They have seen it happen many times and know that it poses no risk. They march carefully on our smooth grass, immediate to the tall grasses of the wetlands, but a far easier walk on turf.

Stop.

The leader, a muscular buck, stands still -- as if catatonic. Followers – the does and the yearlings stay behind the leader – they also stop and stay still as statues.

The leader moves just a few paces. Stops. Stands as catatonic again. Followers stay unmoving, as statues.

The leader moves 20 more feet, then 20 more, then stops, catatonic. Staying and staying and staying and staying still -- catatonic.

Followers had moved 20 feet, then stopped. As statues. They are not advancing and are not moving.

Eventually, the leader moves ahead smoothly and without stopping. Like an all clear.

Followers notice the change and they cavort, run around one another, twitch their ears. They jump. Run together in circles. Move ahead 20-30 feet.

Then. Stop. Wait.

The leader has stopped again, catatonic.

All stop. Watch. Wait. Not even an ear twitch.

Followers staying still as statues.

And then again, an all-clear and tonight's move of the herd proceeds as a stuttering march near the open-space wetlands.

There are no hunters on these lands, just natural predators. But over the years, we've regularly had dogs and coyotes and once even a lone wolf passing through. We've seen new fawns being born -- less than 300 feet from the deck that overlooks the wetlands. And we've seen the mother communicate to the newborn fawn to stay hidden in the grass, not moving until she returns.

To stay safe, the deer have nothing but their instincts, their smarts, their senses, and their behavior. Because the leader of tonight's march has detected something, the followers are deferring to his guidance and maintaining quiet, statue-like stillness until the threat is gone or dismissed. Over many years in the past, deer must have learned this behavior. And those who did learn how to be safe have lived to see another day. Watching this year's herd, it's clear that they will also be survivors.

There are lessons like this in nature. Those deer from days long passed had learned the lessons and survived. Those who didn't were less likely to survive.

WHAT WAS THE PROCESS OF DISCOVERY?

I was watching the deer in their early morning, staccato march. It was a wonderful thing to see of itself.

My discovery was to go beyond just watching and ask myself "*Why* are they doing that?" The lead deer was not forcing the rest of the herd to do things just to exert his power. Rather, he was doing what he could to minimize their detection by some unseen, unknown threat. The herd was exhibiting good followership – because the buck's goal of herd safety was a goal shared by all.

It would be wrong and dangerous to anthropomorphize the deer into a miniature version of our structured work teams. But nature has much to teach us. We should respect the lessons of nature because those who ignore the lessons often pay the ultimate, heavy price.

We know that nature wastes no effort. Nature conserves resources, avoids danger, and thereby lives to see another day.

LESSONS LEARNED:

Lesson 1: Leadership begets followership if there is shared risk. The buck that was leading this small herd was obviously in charge. But he was personally just as motivated to survive ·· whatever risk he'd detected ·· as were the rest of the deer.

Sort of like the pilot who is flying with the passengers in an airplane. The pilot is sharing the risk and his actions are aimed at <u>everyone</u> arriving safely at the destination.

Lesson 2: Short-term conformance is not followership. We may do what's immediately necessary in our structured work environments, just to survive in the near term. But long-term, enthusiastic followership flows from being treated fairly and as a valued person.

HOW YOU CAN DO IT TOO

On occasion, step back from the daily scene and just watch. Ask why. Why are thing happening and can I figure out the rationale? Pay special attention to behavior that happens consistently, without formal instruction, to see if you can detect a pattern of behavior that you can emulate and thereby get better results. Or a pattern that you should avoid, to minimize disruption and waste.

Dr. Sarah Brosnan reported (*NATURE*; VOL 425, pp.297-299; 18 SEPTEMBER 2003) about animal research on *How We Learn Fairness*.

When I first read her article, **Monkeys Reject Unequal Pay** I smiled. Monkeys react just like people to unfairness, becoming angry when they see other monkeys receiving a better reward for doing the same work that the angered monkey is doing. Unfairness is recognized.

I smiled because it reminded me of the angry workers in the biblical **Parable of the Workers in the Vineyard.**
"For the kingdom of heaven is like a landowner who went out early in the morning to hire workers for his vineyard. He agreed to pay them a denarius for the day and sent them into his vineyard.
About nine in the morning he went out and saw others standing in the marketplace doing nothing. He told them, 'You also go and work in my vineyard, and I will pay you whatever is right.' So they went. He went out again about noon and about three in the afternoon and did the same thing. About five in the afternoon he went out and found still others standing around. He asked them, 'Why have you been standing here all day long doing nothing?' 'Because no one has hired us,' they answered. He said to them, 'You also go and work in my vineyard.' When evening came, the owner of the vineyard said to his foreman, 'Call the workers and pay them their wages, beginning with the last ones hired and going on to the first.' **The workers who were hired about five in the afternoon came and each received a denarius. So when those came who were hired first, they expected to receive more. But each one of them also received a denarius. When they received it, they began to grumble against the landowner.** 'These who were hired last worked only one hour,' they said, 'and you have made them equal to us who have borne the burden of the work and the heat of the day.' But he answered one of them, 'I am not being unfair to you, friend. Didn't you agree to work for a denarius? Take your pay and go. I want to give the one who was hired last the same as I gave you. Don't I have the right to do what I want with my own money? Or are you envious because I am generous? **So the last will be first, and the first will be last"** *Matthew 20:1–16*

📖 Formula for Success

THE STORY

When I was at the height of my career, I was sometimes called upon to talk to young people about my career. I would begin my comments by saying that I am going to talk about their careers, not my career. They really didn't care about my career. They did care about their own careers.

Here are the comments I would make to them. I would show them my secret formula for success.

Success = skill (applied ability) + ambition + character + luck.
(SUCCESS = S + A + C + L)

SUCCESS: is peace of mind. Success isn't money, or power, or position. Success is peace of mind. Success is when you are totally content with your life. When you are at peace, you're not aware what you're thinking about. If your car breaks down and you're facing a big repair bill, you're thinking about that. If the Twins are on a long losing streak, you're thinking about that. But when you are totally at ease, you're not aware of what you're thinking about – you're not thinking about anything. That's what success is.

SKILL: You have a lot of talent, and a lot of knowledge, but you have to apply it to the audience you are talking to at the time. That's what skill means to me; the ability to apply your talent and knowledge in a way that is appropriate to your current situation. I bought an Apple One to One contract. The Apple consultants are highly capable technically. But I don't go there to have them be capable on the computer. I go there to learn. And many times, I have to first teach them how to teach in order to get what I need. So, know your audience. Adapt your talent and knowledge to the audience or person you are working with.

AMBITION: Think through what your ambitions are, particularly nowadays, when two career families are common. You need to think that through. There is a give and take in most cases. Nothing says you have to have the ambition to be the next CEO of the company but know what your ambition is. Just be aware that if you are willing to put in a good 40-hour week, but your competitor for a promotion is putting in 80 hours, then other things being equal, that 80-hour person is likely to get the promotion. That surprises people. It shouldn't. When the person who is a workaholic gets the promotion, do you feel bad or do you think 'I accept that; that's what I intended.'

CHARACTER: Character is your reputation. It includes your trustworthiness, but it is also your presence. People will rarely tell you what they think of you, so you have to read the signs so that you are aware of how you are perceived as a person. For example, at a cocktail party, do people come to be near you or do they avoid you? You've got to read the signs. I had a man working for me named Curt. When you called him on the phone, he would answer with a short, abrupt response. One day I said, "Curt, are you aware that your telephone mannerism and your name are the same thing?" And he said, "What do you mean?" I said, "Are you aware that you sound very unfriendly when you pick up the phone? You are curt." He wasn't aware. After that, he used a pleasant greeting.

These things are all your presence. What do people think of you? You need to be aware of that, because it does have an impact on your career.

LUCK: Sometimes you will be lucky. When you are, accept it graciously and modestly. Don't get egotistical. Sometimes you will be unlucky. Don't be a bad loser. Just accept the fact that this time you had an unlucky break. Next time, you might get a lucky break. Don't let it get you down. Just pick yourself up and keep on going. Perseverance is one of the most important ingredients for success.

WHAT WAS THE PROCESS OF DISCOVERY?

I discovered this formula for success through the school of hard knocks. I watched colleagues who had much more talent than I, fail to realize their potential simply because they did not know how to apply their talent at the right time and in the right way. Usually it was because they were too preoccupied with their talent and failed to notice that their co-workers were not impressed.

I always put my family before my career. That probably cost me some promotions because I was not willing to uproot the family and relocate when opportunities came up. In the long run, a happy family life paid off and led to a rewarding career.

It is important to establish your reputation. I always tried act in an ethical manner and had a reputation as the most trustworthy person around. That proved to be an important trademark in my career. Since my bosses trusted me, they gave me much more authority and responsibility than they otherwise would have. This allowed me to be innovative and have a greater impact on the company.

During the course of my career, I only had two bosses who, I felt, treated me unfairly. I reacted by trying to make them look good and earn their respect. On the other hand, I escaped from their departments as soon as I could. Near the end of my career, I worked for a man with whom I was very compatible. It was a lucky break, and I got several promotions from him. I never forgot though how lucky I was because it was pure happenstance that I met him and got the opportunity to work for him.

Some wise person once said:

The happiest people don't **have** the best of everything. They just **make** the best of everything they have.

Source:pixabay.com

LESSONS LEARNED:

Success is peace of mind. Success isn't money, or power, or position. Success is when you are totally content with your life. That requires that you get to know yourself: your skills, your ambitions, and your values. Then practice them to the best of your ability.

HOW YOU CAN DO IT TOO

Follow this formula, and you will be successful. First of all, get to know yourself. Look beyond your résumé. Your résumé documents your education, your work experiences, and your skills. But it doesn't really tell you who you are. What are your goals in life? What are your priorities? Who are you as an individual? These are the questions you need to answer in order to succeed. Rewrite your résumé around each of the four elements of the formula and then practice them. You will have peace of mind: the definition of success.

—Weimerskirch—

Positive Thinking

THE STORY

Honeywell gave us many opportunities to improve our skills. There were numerous workshops on various topics. I remember one workshop in particular. It was a psychological workshop designed to demonstrate the power of positive thinking and conversely, the adverse impact of negative thinking.

We were divided into three teams selected at random from the participants. There was no reason to think that there was any difference in the skill levels of any of the teams. Two of the teams were asked to recommend a solution to a specific business problem. It was a qualitative problem with no definite right or wrong answer. The two teams were asked to analyze the problem, define alternatives, and then recommend a solution.

I was assigned to the third team. Our job was to judge the work of the other two teams. Unbeknownst to the other two teams, we were asked to be very complimentary of one team's work. Not gushy or overt but just subtly complimentary. With the other team, we were asked to be somewhat critical. Again, not obvious, but just mildly critical.

As the two teams reported their findings, we carried out our mission. With the one team, we complimented them on how well they had analyzed the available information, how clear and crisp their decision-making process was, and how their recommended solution seemed to be the best one possible. That team was visibly pleased and beamed with pride.

With the second team, we pointed out that they might have made better use of the information they had to work with, their decision-making process might have been a bit more comprehensive, and that their recommended solution might not have been the best one. That team became somewhat apologetic and acknowledged that they could have done a better job. In reality, the work of the two teams was equal.

WHAT WAS THE PROCESS OF DISCOVERY?

I was amazed at the impact that our comments had on the two teams. We had no authority over them, nor did we have any great credibility. There was no reason why our critique should have had any real impact on them. Yet one team was beaming with pride while the other team was crestfallen.

After this experience, I began to study the impact of attitude on a person's performance and on life in general for that matter. Many books have been written on the subject. The best known is probably The Power of Positive Thinking by Norman Vincent Peale. Everyone who needs to improve their positive thinking would do well to read one of these books.

LESSONS LEARNED:

Positive thinking is a powerful attribute. People should have a high regard for themselves. They should strive to achieve everything they can and then be comfortable with themselves.
Probably the most powerful story of positive thinking is that of Helen Keller. Helen Keller was born blind and deaf. Her teacher, Anne Sullivan, gradually taught her to overcome her extreme handicap of being unable to communicate.

Gradually, through the power of positive thinking, Helen overcame her handicap and went on to become the first blind and deaf person to earn a Bachelor of Arts degree.

Eventually she became one of the world's leading humanitarians.

Helen Keller
Source: Wikimedia Commons

Helen Keller stated her philosophy of life this way: *"I have for many years endeavored to make this vital truth clear; and still people marvel when I tell them that I am happy. They imagine that my limitations weigh heavily upon my spirit, and chain me to the rock of despair. Yet, it seems to me, happiness has very little to do with the senses.*

If we make up our minds that this is a drab and purposeless universe, it will be that, and nothing else. On the other hand, if we believe that the earth is ours, and that the sun and moon hang in the sky for our delight, there will be joy upon the hills and gladness in the fields because the Artist in our souls glorifies creation. Surely, it gives dignity to life to believe that we are born into this world for noble ends, and that we have a higher destiny than can be accomplished within the narrow limits of this physical life." ~ *Helen Keller*

HOW YOU CAN DO IT TOO

Set your own standards of performance. Don't let other people's opinions have any great influence on you. Listen to other people's opinions and suggestions so that you take advantage of opportunities to learn and improve but don't let those opinions and suggestions affect your attitude or your regard for yourself. Keep a positive attitude. Have a high regard for yourself. Think positively. Seek opportunities to improve but don't let other people's opinions diminish your self-respect.

It is important to realize that positive thinking is not arrogance. Everyone has opportunities to improve. The arrogant person ignores any advice and lacks the self-confidence to improve. The positive thinking person has the self-confidence to listen to advice and search for opportunities to improve.

When you experience a setback in life, as you inevitably will, write it off as an anomaly. Pick yourself up and go on thinking positively. Use every challenge as an opportunity to improve.
People are happiest when they achieve everything they are capable of achieving and then accept their limitations. Not everyone is destined to be a movie star or an all-star athlete.

When you see a brilliant athletic performance, artistic performance, or outstanding technological achievement be amazed and enjoy. Then, ask, "How did they do that?" to see if their performance gives you a hint at something you can personally do to be even better than you are now. See if that performance can inspire you to heights beyond what you thought you could achieve.

But, in the end, be comfortable with yourself. The fulfillment comes in doing the best you can at whatever you try.

—Weimerskirch—

📖 What do you do after you don't have a business card?

THE STORY

After I reached the age of 60, I found that many of my colleagues were retiring. More and more, I began to feel like the "old man." But I dreaded the thought of retirement. I loved my job and had no idea what I would do in retirement. I really had no hobbies. Many of us are defined by our careers, perhaps more than we should be. We spend our careers setting objectives, meeting challenges, and achieving new heights. I worried about what life would be like once that environment disappeared. Where would I find fulfillment in life?

During most of my career, I kept this picture of a mountain in my office.

I would imagine that I am climbing that mountain trying to achieve new heights. Sometimes, I would look up to the top of the mountain and see that I have a long way to go to the top. Other times, I would look down and see that I had come a long way too. But each day I would cling to the side of the mountain trying to get a few steps higher. I felt a need to achieve and I felt that if I retired, I would not be achieving anything anymore.

But I had promised my wife that I would retire at 65 whether I wanted to or not. I spent a lot of time studying retirement. All the advice seemed to deal with what to do with my time after I was retired. A friend of mine told me, "Arnie, when it comes time to retire, you will know it." It just didn't seem like the right time.

In my case, retirement came automatically at age 63 1/2. Honeywell merged with Allied Signal and moved its headquarters to New Jersey. I was eligible for full retirement and had a generous severance package. I wasn't about to move to New Jersey, so I retired.

After retirement, I decided to volunteer. I had been fortunate in my career and I felt like I owed something back to society. I quickly found that I was volunteering with 5 organizations. One day, I had 5 meetings, one with each organization. I thought, "This is ridiculous. I am running from one meeting to another and doing nobody any good." So, I withdrew from those organizations and joined the University of St. Thomas to help them form a School of Engineering. I accepted some nominal compensation because that required that I make a contribution. I had some responsibilities. I worked about half time.

We succeeded in officially establishing the School of Engineering in 2004. I continued to work for the School of Engineering for several more years. Then I transferred to the Veritas Institute at the University of St. Thomas College of Business. We worked in the area of corporate social responsibility. I continued to work there part-time until I was 82 years old.

WHAT WAS THE PROCESS OF DISCOVERY?

I discovered that all the advice about using my time was wrong. There was no problem filling my time. The important thing to consider in retirement is socialization. A person's job is a very important part of their socialization even for those people who hate their job. It is very fulfilling to work with respected colleagues when you enjoy your job. If you hate your job, you have the opportunity to vent your frustrations or worries to your colleagues who give you a sympathetic ear. My job at St. Thomas afforded me a great socialization opportunity and still gave me an opportunity to achieve.

I still keep that picture of the mountain in my office at home. I still feel a need to achieve, but there are many ways to do that. Writing these articles is one of them. I find though that the need to achieve gradually diminishes as I age.

But we are all different. My friends have taken many different paths in life after retirement. One friend retired from his job abruptly, moved to Florida with his wife and plays golf or tennis virtually every day. Another friend and his wife sold their house, bought a motor home and spend their time travelling the country and volunteering at national parks. There are many different ways to fill your time. The common thread is socialization.

LESSONS LEARNED:

There are two basic principles of retirement:
1. Get to know yourself
2. Socialization is the most important consideration in retirement.

Most people don't ever get to know themselves at the core. People think of themselves in terms of their education, their career and their families. They don't think about their value system, their need for association or their aspirations. Retirement requires one to think about those things.

Everyone has a need to connect with other human beings. But that need varies greatly by individual. Some people need to be with other people much of the time. Others need a great deal of privacy. Likewise, some people have a great need to achieve. Others do not. Finding the right balance between socialization and achievement is the key to a happy retirement.

Those are the two basic principles. There are several other subsidiary principles that are interrelated. They may or may not apply to everyone because we are all different. They may serve as helpful hints when considering retirement.

1. Take advantage of what you know not what you do
   - During the course of a career, people acquire a great deal of knowledge that one cannot learn from a textbook. That knowledge is helpful to those who have less experience. The strategy should be to free up one's time while still applying the knowledge built up over the years. In retirement, a person's time should be much more flexible.

2. A good retirement is when your mind and your body can be in two different places
   - During their career, most people are required to be present on the job. Even for those who work from home, they are required to be there. But if a person can use what they know not what they do, they can be anywhere. For

example, I winter in Florida in the warm sunshine, but my mind is on my work at the University of St. Thomas. From Florida I could use my knowledge to benefit St. Thomas in Minneapolis.

3. Exercise is very important
   - The human body was made to work. Both physical and mental exercise is very important for a good retirement. Evidence suggests that exercise is a key to avoiding or at least delaying Alzheimer's disease. Too many people look at retirement as an opportunity to sit back and do nothing. They rapidly deteriorate both physically and mentally. That is not a fulfilling retirement.

4. There are several retirements
   - Retirement is a journey, not a destination. The need to achieve gradually diminishes as one grows older. The need for socialization also diminishes as one grows older. There is no need to make long range plans for retirement. Things can always change. An ideal retirement would allow for flexible hours on the job diminishing gradually over time. Volunteering is a great way to get that flexibility while still providing adequate socialization.

HOW YOU CAN DO IT TOO

If you were being interviewed for a job, you would probably talk about your education, your work experiences and your family. But do you really know yourself? What is really important to you? What are you really like on the inside? What fulfills you?

If you are contemplating retirement, get to know yourself. Think through the type of socialization you need. How much private time do you need? How much of the time do you have a need to be with people? What socialization do you get on your job? How will you replace it once you retire? What do you like to do in your spare time? What is your need to achieve? How will you replace that in your retirement?

If you answered those questions honestly, you would discover that you are different from everyone else. No one else is like you. So, don't try to fit yourself into a cookie cutter formula for your retirement. Tailor your retirement largely based on your socialization needs. You can always find ways to meet your need to achieve and fill your time.

—Weimerskirch—

Chapter 02
Following the Golden Rule

📖   Flying can be fun, or not

THE STORY

My company did a very high volume of business travel with the airline, so employees received preferential seating in coach. That is, those traveling in coach were assigned seats in the front part of the coach section. Sort of like the "comfort seat" arrangements airlines started using – and charging extra for -- in the early-2000s.

That front part of coach was usually filled with adults who were traveling as part of their job, trying to do work during the flight. It was much quieter and less distracting than other parts of coach class where families were seated, with associated sounds of noisy babies and constant child movement.

This was a KLM aircraft, flying in a code sharing arrangement with Northwest. The flight crew and flight attendants were Dutch, and the aircraft configuration was unique to KLM preferences. It was a Boeing 747.

I was bound for a long trip to Europe and even though I wasn't in business class, I was given an excellent seat in the front part of the coach section. My row of coach seats was next to the 747 boarding door and consequently had a several feet of legroom between us and the wall where business class seating started.

A very comfortable seat. My seatmates were chit-chatting with *get-to-know-you* small talk. We still had about 30-minutes before the doors would be closed and we would be taking off.

My seat was comfortable, but the small talk faded and then stopped because behind me was a loud, whiney, pushy, malcontent brat of a man making a non-stop, huge fuss. He was literally whining -- like a child deprived of a cookie -- that his company **ALWAYS** secured one of those preferred seats when he flew to Europe. He voiced loudly and repeatedly that KLM had to do something because the people in the first row of coach were sitting in HIS seats. We were very irritated with the whining and astonished that a businessman traveler was acting this way.

I think we all wanted to turn around and tell him to "use your inside voice."

Started in 1926, Northwest Airlines was a major airline, headquartered in Minneapolis, Minnesota until Northwest merged with Delta Airlines in 2008.

Did you know that Northwest had a special room at the Minneapolis-St. Paul airport for high volume companies? It was in the airport check-in area, behind a special, non-labeled door. Your company travel office had to alert you that it was there for your use. It wasn't quite like a "speakeasy", secret entrance used by illicit bars during Prohibition, but it did make one feel special.

Employees whose companies did a very high volume of business with Northwest were invited to use the special room for their frequent-flier, business fliers.

The flight attendants tried to calm his whines. But he kept up with his selfish demands that one of us be moved so HE could sit where HE was supposed to be sitting. He was NOT supposed to be sitting in the "crummy second row coach seats!"

Part of the KLM flight attendants' attempts to stop his whining was to offer him a seat in their aircraft's galley area. A single, First-Class sized seat in their galley area with LOTS of legroom. He refused. He wanted HIS seat in the first row. The whines and demands continued.

We were all becoming very tired of his tirade and knew that an eight-hour flight with his non-stop, childish whines would be miserable. So, I stood up, found the flight attendant and told her that I would stay in my seat for takeoff, but that he could then sit in my seat and I'd sit in the galley seat until it was time to land. They were relieved and said "Yes."

I returned to his row, and something very unusual for me, I told him aloud that he was a rude, selfish baby and that he could have my seat after takeoff and for the flight. But, when it was time to land, I'd be back, and he'd have to return to his original seat behind me for the landing. He continued whining a whimper that it just wasn't right, that I had HIS seat, but that my plan was OK.

We took off. The bell rang to say we'd cleared 10,000 feet, and soon the seat belt sign was turned off. I stood up, grabbed my things, and told him he could have my seat. He stopped whining, and though ostracized with silence by his seatmates, he sat down in "HIS" seat.

Meanwhile, I followed the flight attendant to the galley area. On that KLM 747, the galley was directly on the side of the fuselage – a long room. Passengers seated in the coach cabin, by the galley, are seated by the wall of the galley on their right and don't have a window view.

My seat in the galley – for the duration of the flight – was a huge, wide, comfortable, first-class reclining seat at the forward end of the plane, I could watch everything but be out of the way of everyone. There were wide ledges on both sides to store my materials. I had made multiple flights in business class and this seat had everything you'd expect in business or first-class.

But the treat was to spend eight hours watching and interacting with the crew. KLM crews are always the best, but this was even more, watching them at work with their friends. They sat down near me on their breaks and shared favorite stories from The Netherlands where they grew up, where they went to school, events at family gatherings, and funny and embarrassing things they'd done while growing up. It was much like a family reunion where you meet relatives whose names you knew but whom you had seldom actually met. They asked where I was going in Holland and Germany and wrote down a short list of best places that the "locals" knew to be outstanding but were not in the tourist books. This was long before Yelp and TripAdvisor and it felt like a best friend telling secrets about best places that tourists would otherwise never learn about.

The captain came back for coffee and we had a most interesting conversation about the state of commercial flying and what he planned to do after retiring. He thanked me for defusing the situation with the whiner who was now sitting in my seat. The flight attendant brought me a menu to choose anything on the first-class menu, including multiple offerings for dessert.

Then, the BOLS houses. A popular souvenir of a first-class flight on KLM were small, Dutch-style, porcelain houses, just inches high, and filled with Dutch Genever liqueur. The attendants gave me several little houses – normally only available if served to customers in business class -- as a Thank You.

Delft Blue houses are presented to Business and Royal Class travelers on KLM flights. KLM started this in 1952. As of 2017, 97 different Delft Blue houses have been issued. The miniature houses are actually bottles – cork and a seal on the top, and are filled with Dutch Genever, 35% alcohol.

Photo by John Fechter

It was probably the most enjoyable flight of the hundreds I have made in over 45+ years. The three, little bottles are still on a bookshelf at home, and still make me smile when I think of the people I met on that flight.

Visiting with the captain. Huge seat. Pampered by everyone! Heard stories of their families. Pictures of their kids. Had a quiet place to do my homework.

Learned about and visited some best places in Amsterdam, Maastricht, and Aachen for a meal and sightseeing...
And the dessert on my trip was to walk back to my originally assigned seat just before starting to land and telling the loud whiner "Back to your assigned seat." A blossoming wave of smiles greeted me from seatmates who had received a reprieve for eight hours of his disgusting whines.

WHAT WAS THE PROCESS OF DISCOVERY?

It wasn't my job to stop the whiner or appease his childlike behavior. But I was definitely impacted by a disruptive-situation that was going to ruin a long, 8-hour flight and have me arrive in Europe tired and in a foul mood.
I addressed the symptom (the whiney brat) and accepted the offer they had made to him. I didn't fix the problem – he's probably still whining his way through life – but I did take action to minimize the problem.

After the flight, I realized how special it had become as I joined "their space." I have a lifelong affection now for KLM and its people.

LESSONS LEARNED:

1. The Golden Rule rules. "Do unto others, as you would have others do unto you." But the whiny brat was not the one I was "doing unto." No, "the others" were the sincere and friendly flight attendants trying to make things work for all of us.

2. KLM personnel, in my experience, were always direct, but gracious and friendly, and honest to a fault. So, when they offered what they described to the whiney brat as "a great alternative seat in their galley" I believed them. It didn't make any sense that they would have offered an inferior seating alternative that put the whiner in their flight-long work and break area, unless it truly was fantastic. He didn't take it. I did. It was more than fantastic.

HOW YOU CAN DO IT TOO

Be mindful as much as possible.

Live -- aware of the moment. If someone needs help and you can help, then do it.

I live with an awareness of cause → effect. If you aren't getting the effects (the results) you want or expect, ask what needs to be changed in the collection of causes, and then make the changes so the modified causes are working properly to achieve the effects you seek.

If you are in a management position, you can change the world if you get off the spectator's bench and offer help to people who are living with a process that delivers inferior results. Individuals are seldom empowered to personally change the process, but with management support it can be done.

—Fechter—

Friendliness is free

THE STORY

I had just returned from Europe on a late Friday afternoon flight. Since I had commitments Monday morning, I went to my office to get the mail to see if anything required immediate action. When I got there, on my desk I found a broken thermostat and a letter from a woman in Seattle. The woman was complaining that the thermostat didn't work, and it increased her heating bill. The letter said she had been treated rudely by the company representative in charge of her account and had gotten no satisfaction of her complaint. She felt strongly enough about the matter that she wrote a letter to me as Vice President of Quality for the company.

I called her up and identified myself. Her first comment was "It is 8:00 on a Friday night in Minneapolis. What are you doing in your office?" I explained why I was in my office and that I was concerned about her situation. I said "Right now you are frustrated with my company. What do I have to do to turn you around so that you will brag about my company?" She said, "All I really want is for someone to listen to me and to pay my additional heating cost." It was only a few dollars. I told her I would get a check in the mail to her on Monday. She thanked me for listening to her concern and for being kind to her. I said, "Now will you go around bragging about my company?" She said she would. That's all it took.

On another occasion, I received a letter from a woman in New Jersey. She too complained that she had been treated rudely by the company representative. Again, I said, "What do I have to do to get you to brag about my company?" She said she really didn't want anything except to have someone listen to her concerns. So, I listened to her tell me how she had been treated badly by the company representative. I explained that that is not typical of my company and that I was very sorry for the way she had been treated. The conversation went on for a while. Finally, she said "I hardly know you, but you seem so friendly. Can I adopt you?" I suggested that she might want to check into my spending habits before she did that. But in the end, she said she would now brag about my company.

WHAT WAS THE PROCESS OF DISCOVERY?

In seminars that I had attended and in my work experiences, I learned of about the importance of active listening. Active listening is the art of taking time to really understand what the other person is trying to tell you. Usually in a conversation, people are only half listening while they think of what they are going to say next. Customers then get the impression that you don't really care about them and are left unfulfilled.

I also learned that, in the whole realm of customer relationships, friendliness is probably the most important factor. Many times, it is more important than the product or service itself and it makes price less important.

LESSONS LEARNED:

Friendliness is free. It doesn't cost anything to be pleasant, but it makes all the difference in the world.

HOW YOU CAN DO IT TOO

Anyone can be friendly. It is a trait that anyone can learn. Any time you encounter another person (which is frequently) do or say something to make them feel good about themselves. It will pay big dividends.

—Weimerskirch—

The friendliest place we've ever lived

Cuyahoga River – a success story

The Cuyahoga River in Northeast Ohio runs through Cleveland before emptying into Lake Erie. In mid-1900s Cleveland emerged as a major manufacturing center. But with limited controls about what could be dumped into the river, it became heavily affected by industrial pollution; it "caught fire" 13 times, most famously in June 1969. That latest *burning Cuyahoga* incident led to a national outcry, which helped spur the American environmental movement and build support for creation of the Environmental Protection Agency (EPA). President Richard Nixon proposed establishing the EPA on July 1970; it began operation in early December 1970, after Nixon signed an executive order.

In December 1970 a federal grand jury started an investigation of water pollution allegedly being caused by about 12 companies in northeastern Ohio -- the first grand jury investigation of water pollution in the area.

Since 1970, the Cuyahoga river has been extensively cleaned up through efforts by Cleveland's city government and the Ohio Environmental Protection Agency (OEPA). **In 2019, the American Rivers conservation association named the Cuyahoga "River of the Year" in honor of "50 years of environmental resurgence."**

From multiple sources at Wikipedkia.com

THE STORY

Maybe it was the world-famous news story about Cleveland's Cuyahoga River burning, as a persistent slick of oil and chemicals floating on the river caught fire in 1969? Nobody in Cleveland was "putting on airs" after that humbling experience. Or perhaps it was always a friendly place? I think the latter; we lived there from 1992-1998 and loved it!

When we moved to Cleveland, we had a preconceived notion of what the city might be like. What we found was something quite different. Not what we expected; it was better than what we expected. And what made it better were features that weren't even on the list of expectations we had brought with us.

Our Cleveland experiences began with a house-hunting trip after accepting a position at Society Bank. During that trip we found it all but impossible to make dinner reservations downtown. It was late October and the city was celebrating "Sweetest Day," an event originally developed by candy makers in Cleveland in the 1920s. It was a well-established *"mini St. Valentine's Day"* by the time we arrived in town, searching for our new home.

With cards, candy, flowers, treats, and other expressions of love exchanged during the day, couples of all ages had also made dinner plans to celebrate. Who could complain about no room at restaurants when one understood why everywhere was full?

We liked the entire Cleveland area because people took time to make eye contact. Taxi drivers in every city talk to their fares in the back seat. Too often, one hears mostly about political issues and a "throw the bums out" conclusion. But in Cleveland it was inquiries about family or bragging about their youngsters rather than complaints about city hall or "the man" as usually heard in other cities. Bank tellers. Downtowners. Blue collar workers. Executives. Friends, and visitors. All having lunch together at the Cleveland Arcade (I was a fan of the Greek Restaurant). Clerks at the shopping malls.

People exuded a friendly spirit – to everyone. Much like the caring and attention one felt with New

Yorkers when visiting their city years later after
9/11.

I was working with tellers at the downtown Society
Bank building. Beautiful artwork, high, high
ceilings, golden chandeliers, polished marble all
around us. One day, when I asked about customer
service, several tellers said I MUST talk to the teller
who had recently taken care of the elderly man with
his coins. I did.

The teller was friendly, but shy. The story was about
an elderly man who had stood in line, patiently
awaiting the next teller. When it was his turn, he
walked up to her with a cloth bag filled with coins.
She emptied the bag and counted the total –
something around $300. Many of the coins were still
shiny though with long-ago dates on them.

She asked casually where they came from. And with
a bittersweet smile he told her they were his coin
collection. His wife needed surgery and he didn't
have the money to pay the bills, so he was selling
things and decided to trade in his coin collection for
cash. She asked him to have a seat while she made a
call.

Across the street and down the block from Public
Square was the Cleveland Arcade. (It originally
opened as the first indoor shopping center in
America in 1890 and later became a shopping area
and a Hyatt Regency hotel.)

Inside the Cleveland Arcade was a coin dealer. The
teller asked him to come over to the bank to look at a
coin collection. He did and looked carefully through
the elderly gentleman's collection. He appraised its
value far, far above the nominal cash value of about
$300. He made the gentleman an offer, which was
accepted with smiles and a hearty "Thank You."

This was friendliness and compassion in action. She knew the collection's value was far more than its $300 face value. She could have paid him $300 from her own wallet, deposited that into his account and later sold the collection herself, profiting from its real value. After all, $300 was all that he was expecting.

But she didn't.

Instead, she did the right thing. She found the coin

> Upon leaving Cleveland's downtown Arcade mid-winter, an elderly woman's wheelchair slipped on the icy sidewalk and she fell out of her chair. Immediately, other passers-by and I rushed over to help her get back into her wheelchair. She was shaken up but otherwise OK and we wished her well and dispersed. A few days later, a Black man who'd been there and had helped, saw me again at the Arcade, having lunch. He came over with the broadest smile and a tear in his eye to say *Thanks*. The elderly woman was also Black, and the man said that because of past problems he had not expected White people to help so quickly and enthusiastically. But they had. He was beaming and commented that this was a new day and the future looked bright.

dealer and working together the teller and the coin dealer enabled the man to sell the collection for its true value, to help pay the upcoming medical bills. Values. They still matter. And we delight when behaviors show our better side values are alive and well in everyday life.

WHAT WAS THE PROCESS OF DISCOVERY?

I learned about the compassionate teller by "going to the Gemba", to where the work was being done.

My formal responsibility was senior vice president for quality. To do that job well I needed to see and understand the day-to-day processes in use, not through formal presentations with fancy slides and numbers – those I had already received. Instead, I needed to watch from a distance, close enough to see what was happening, but far enough away that I wasn't becoming part of the process.

The tellers were aware of me and why I was there periodically, walking through the downtown bank's customer area. Together, we'd found and fixed some problems and acted on some of their suggestions that surfaced through discussions and questions during my walk-throughs. And living up to Cleveland's reputation for eye-to-eye contact and friendliness, the tellers alerted me to the coin collection teller experience. Today, we'd call that a best practice. But at the time, it was a "story you have to hear." Shared with pride and pleasure after neighboring tellers had seen it happen.

LESSONS LEARNED:

People are people. And people delight when their people-to-people experiences echo their own personal values. Instead of seeing a banking transaction, the teller saw a person, understood his dilemma, and took an extra step to ensure the best outcome. Hers was a small, extra action that produced results far beyond a basic banking transaction. That's the thing about values. They don't prescribe exactly what to do. Values, rather than prescriptive rules and regulations, show us a bright standard through which we can look at our immediate circumstances and know the right thing to do.

HOW YOU CAN DO IT TOO

Values. If you have a strict mercantilist perspective, value is the financial gain you can make from transactions. That's where "things" have value. But to me, that's not the world of values. No, values are the foundation of my world – the beliefs and expectations I have about life – be honest, tell the truth, "Do unto others as I would have them do unto me", don't waste time, don't waste life, don't waste things, etc. Whatever I do, I don't want my actions to conflict with my values. It's not "what can I get away with?" Rather, it is "what is the right thing to do?"

If you take the time to think them through, and say them aloud, your values give you confidence and pleasure to meet life's daily challenges. And if you haven't thought through things to develop a list of your values, use the performance standard, "what is the right thing to do?" One good news aspect about bad news is that we are hearing about the bad news **because** it conflicts so much with our values – people are saying aloud, that is NOT OK.

The "always on guard" security slogan of today is "If you see something, say something." It suggests that if you see something suspicious, you should alert the authorities, so they can check it out and take action if necessary. My perspective on the slogan is -- if you see something that shows values in practice, *say something so others can be heartened and keep putting their own values into action. Or, if you see something that conflicts with values, say something so others know that the conflicting behavior should be challenged.*

—Fechter—

📖 Why didn't you pound the counter?

THE STORY

After a short trip to The Netherlands, my wife and I were back at Amsterdam's Airport Schiphol (in my opinion, one of the best airports in the world). We were seeking our gate so we could check in and receive our boarding passes. It had been a fun holiday in a very nice part of the world.

The concourse was peaceful and bright as people gathered at their gates, casually arranging their carry-on items before boarding. However, as we approached our own gate area it was a noisy, dysfunctional mess. All was chaos. Loud voices. Angry scowls. Rudeness dripping from the air. Some tears.

What had happened?

Several hours after takeoff a KLM 747 had just returned to Schiphol due to mechanical problems – passengers on the cancelled flight were disembarking at our gate. There were hundreds of passengers, cheek to jowl as people from the returned flight mixed with people like us who were trying to get boarding passes for our own 747 flight. Tempers flared. Niceties were gone.

Sounding almost like an opera, a chorus of people were simultaneously yelling at the several KLM clerks, pounding the countertop, waving and shoving forward their tickets, boarding passes, and paperwork -- demanding that the clerks answer the question and command, "Don't you know who I am? KLM better get me on this next flight!"

The problem was obvious – more passengers in the gate area than a single 747 could hold. There were nearly as many of us scheduled on the next flight as the number who had just disembarked from the returned flight. There was simply not enough room on our 747 to accommodate everyone scheduled on our flight plus those who had just returned.

As our departure time approached, people were becoming ever more frantic. The yelling was louder. The pounding was harder. The clerks gave people pieces of paper with information about upcoming or alternative flights, but they were giving out few boarding passes.

"Next?" The KLM clerks appeared calm but were starting to present a steady, pink flush in their face and neck from the non-stop, rude, and threatening pressure to fix a problem that had no fix.

As we entered the middle of the gate area, my wife felt the urgency in the air. "Tell them you're a million-mile flier. You'll have to push harder than everyone else or we'll be stuck here for a day or two." I replied that I was sure there were piles of platinum, gold, and silver frequent fliers in the queue. "Wait here."

She waited pensively, leaning on a huge column near the wall of the boarding area.

The long, long line of yelling, vein-popping customers in front of me was nearly gone when it became my turn. Stepping up to a KLM clerk who had been enduring the scolding passengers, I said "People shouldn't be treating you like this. It's not a problem you can fix. Do what you can for us. We're OK." I smiled, gave her the tickets, and she took a long breath, gathered her thoughts, and said quietly, "Thanks. I'll call you if I can do anything."
No pounding the counter. No yelling.

We waited.

And waited.

More yelling and pounding by customers who intermittently returned to the counter. Then, gate personnel started calling the names of people whose boarding passes and seat assignments were ready. People walked up, exchanged the information paper they'd been given earlier, and received boarding passes. Each lucky soul went by the machine to scan the boarding pass, and then walked down the jetway to the waiting 747. They had a seat! Some were disembarked passengers from the returned flight. Others were people scheduled for this flight.

By this time, many disembarked passengers who knew they would not be rebooked to this flight had already left for other gates to find alternative flights -- eventually flying to their destination city though not via their original route. The huge crowd of anxious passengers-to-be was thinning, still murmuring with frustration. My wife was growing concerned again. "You should have pushed harder. We'll probably never get on."

The crowd thinned, and by now it was obvious that almost everyone who was going to be on the immediate flight was already on board. Just a few more to go.

We waited. I said to my wife, "Well, we'll get another chance to visit Amsterdam this afternoon." I smiled and laughed. She didn't. And she pursed her lips in worry.

The clock moved ever so slowly.

Only a very few passengers were still waiting. Almost everyone had either been accommodated on other flights, had left after deciding to take a flight tomorrow, or perhaps had given up and gone on their own to seek alternatives. Then, the clerk made eye contact with me and subtly motioned with her head for us to come over. She handed us two boarding passes, saying quietly, "Board now please. Don't say a word until you land. And thank you for your kindness."

We said a sincere thanks, and they closed the door behind us because we were the last two to get on the flight. My wife was floating, relieved that we were on the plane as planned. I looked down at the boarding passes. I smiled, saying nothing. The clerk had done what she could. We were seated in the first-class bubble on the top of the 747, where there were only 16 seats, very large and very comfortable. I'd been seated there on previous business class travels and it was always a delightful flight from that perch.

The KLM clerk had treated us well, delighted us, and rescued us. Why? Because it was in her nature to help everyone – even while knowing she couldn't help them all. And, I believe that she treated us well because we had treated her as an equal, our peer, with kindness and patience, as she dealt with a horde of screaming, infantile, angry, rude, hostile, threatening people. It was the golden rule in practice, both of us had obeyed the rule, "Do unto others as you would have others do unto you."

KLM people – on the ground or onboard ·· were always real people who made eye contact with each of us and welcomed us warmly as new friends who were entering *their* home. After the kindness of the abused clerk at Schiphol, I put KLM on the top of my short list – **in ink**.

In November 2010, a man was in queue to purchase a lottery ticket in The Philippines. It was worth a fortune: 741,000,000 pesos, about $17 million.

He was pushed aside by a woman trying to get ahead of him. He backed away and let her by. Then, letting the system choose his numbers, he purchased what became the winning ticket. He won the fortune! Was karma at work?

Although there is no proof, many people believe the phrase "what goes around comes around." That is, treat people nicely and the world will treat you nicely as well, But, treat people badly, and after a time the world will "come around" and treat you badly in kind.

Karma is a spiritual principle associated with the concept of rebirths; it is described as performing in a similar fashion to "what goes around comes around."

That is: "Good intent and good deeds contribute to good karma and happier rebirths, while bad intent and bad deeds contribute to bad karma and bad rebirths." https://en.wikipedia.org/wiki/Karma

WHAT WAS THE PROCESS OF DISCOVERY?

Values vs. policy vs. procedures...

Customer facing people in every business unfortunately encounter customers who are tired, frustrated, weary, sick, or otherwise impaired. In addition to those things that cause customers to behave poorly, some customers are bullies, narcissistic, never learned manners, or don't understand or believe that without exception other people deserve recognition and respect, no matter what their station in life.

We all know that.

My behavior with the KLM clerk was pleasant and respectful. We mostly do that. But I realized later that what I did differently than others was to show her respect. My comments recognized that she was trying to do an impossible task, and do it with a smile, for people whose behavior was demeaning and disrespectful to her. My comments were said aloud to her and within earshot of others -- **"People shouldn't be treating you like this. It's not a problem you can fix. Do what you can for us. We're OK."**

LESSONS LEARNED:

I believe that a key to better behavior by all is to say it aloud when someone is not being treated as they should be. Good behavior does not become a societal norm unless bad behavior is noted in real time and critiqued as unacceptable. Not as a *goodie-two-shoes*, but as people respecting people.
People are people. Their roles may change – but they remain people. Just like you. Just like me.

HOW YOU CAN DO IT TOO

"If you see something, say something" doesn't just apply to terrorism threats. If you see something that is not right, say something. And, if you see something that is very right, say something.
For many, many reasons, social interactions in today's world can feel frayed and frantic.

It's an old but proven standard that we should all use: "Do unto others as you would have others do unto you."

I recall standing in line for some airport fast-food when a well-dressed customer berated the clerk as stupid and slow while she made his sandwich. Both were strangers to one another. We other strangers in line all saw and heard it. We hadn't yet said anything, but the next customer in line – also a well-dressed stranger to us all -- said aloud to the bully that he was being rude and insulting and that he needed to apologize to her. The rude person's face flushed, he sputtered, but then he stopped immediately as other customers in line applauded his put-down.

If you see something, say something.

—Fechter—

Chapter 03
Simplifying Daily Life

Angry ranchers in the ranger's office

THE STORY

At the north end of Montana's Helena Valley lies *The Sleeping Giant*. Initially named the Bear Tooth formation it acquired a new name several years after an earthquake in the late 1800s that collapsed a massive stone outcropping and changed the shape. An article in Helena's *Independent Record* newspaper in 1893 highlighted that the mountains now looked like a giant man sleeping on the horizon.

The Sleeping Giant

Photo by John Fechter

During a springtime trip, my wife and I were visiting our hometown, Helena, Montana.

Driving north toward the Sleeping Giant, I pointed to the right, at the Helena District Ranger's office and the U.S Forest Service equipment yard next to the highway. The yard was once open and spacious but is now filled with trucks, culverts, logs, forest fire-fighting gear, campground construction supplies, and related materials.

A drawknife is commonly used to remove large slices of wood for flat faceted work, **to debark trees**, or to create roughly rounded or cylindrical billets for further work on a lathe, or it can shave like a spokeshave plane, where finer finishing is less of concern than a rapid result.

The thin blade lends itself to create complex concave or convex curves.
https://en.wikipedia.org/wiki/Drawknife

Years ago, I had started working there as a college student. On my first day of work I was assigned the task of stripping bark from pine tree logs, so they could be used for signposts, fencing, and campgrounds. The task was easy, light exercise, and enjoyable – working under blue skies, outside, pulling a draw knife toward myself, rotating the log, continuing with the draw knife, rotating, and then starting a new log. And it came with a clear, visual metric – a large pile of logs smelling like a forest -- of what I'd accomplished during the day. Before that summer job, I'd spent too much sedentary time inside at college. This outdoor job with the smell of fresh pine was a perfect alternative. They say that one of our most persistent memories are of smells – and the pine smell is at the top of my short list of delightful smells.

Fire suppression is an important service provided by the U.S. Forest Service, especially in western parts of the United States. Most districts are staffed with a mix of several year-round personnel and a larger group of summer-only employees available to respond quickly when a fire breaks out. And between fires, while standing at the ready, those same crews make productive use of "down-time" when they are not needed for fire suppression.

Productive use of "down-time" covers safety training, maintenance of campgrounds, building fence, planting seedlings in harvested or fire-cleared parts of the forest, etc.

Other tasks included daily patrols through public access areas where campground fires and firepits may have been abandoned but improperly extinguished. On other days, we would be cutting timber in areas where logging has been done but irregular and damaged logs needed to be cleared before the area is re-seeded or re-planted, etc.

In addition to those kinds of daily tasks and training, summer employees (often college students on a summer break from school) learn many life lessons through watching and listening as the ranger and full-time staff plan, hear from forest users, authorize permits, and such.

Driving by the ranger's office in May 2019, I recalled the following life lesson:

Our summer crew has just entered a break room for lunch. We noticed that something different was happening outside – a number of pickup trucks were pulling in. Usually, individual trucks would pull in a few times a day as people obtained permits and had other business with the ranger's office.

Today, one by one, ranchers stepped out of their dusty trucks, put on their well-worn cowboy hats, planted their cowboy boots firmly into the gravel by their truck, and then start walking firmly and forcefully toward the building, some slamming their truck door to punctuate their presence.

The ranger's administrative assistant couldn't do much except point the newcomers to the ranger's office where loud, emphatic, red-faced, statements were being made. It was a heated, unstructured, and frustrating collection of noise and confusion.

Why the anger? Why the confrontation? What had happened?

Turns out that each rancher had recently received notice in the mail that they did not have permission to graze their cattle in the district's National Forest this summer. They had regularly received such permission in the past and they were counting on continued access now and for the future.

In fact, each was waving a piece of paper with U.S. Forest Service logos and signatures on it. Yet each was denied continued access. Why?

We watched and heard the episode from the nearby break room. When all the commotion quieted down, and after the ranchers had stormed out, their trucks spitting gravel with their departure, the ranger came into the break room to grab a cup of coffee, sit down, and decompress.

He shared the facts and we learned a tiny lesson with lifelong impact to our lives.

When it comes to paperwork, draft or final version -- Date everything.

Everything?

Everything!

Over the years, starting with just a few ranchers, multiple grazing permits had been issued by Forest Service staff, previous rangers, and others. But many permits did not note who issued the permit, the date it was issued, or the end date noted. And no annual, summer inventory of permitted areas was maintained in the office. The forest had become over-subscribed with more cattle than the available grazing land could support. The situation couldn't continue; if the oversubscribed cattle were all allowed to graze, the grass available was insufficient to handle them all.

The meeting had been loud, frightening, and frustrating for all. No one left happy. We weren't privy to how other lands were made available that summer and how land was allotted in the future, but the ranger made it clear that the many problems could have been avoided if only the permitting process was properly documented.

WHAT WAS THE PROCESS OF DISCOVERY?

As summer-time college students we were blessed with the opportunity to work **and learn.** The wisdom of "old hands" would come out as war stories during breaks, during lunches, and as we worked together in quiet times and during the organized chaos of fighting forest fires. We had a lot of time to talk about these things as we drove to and from fire locations in that part of Montana.

And we learned.

WE NOTED THREE LIFE LESSONS:

1. All work can be defined as a process. But if the process isn't documented it changes in subtle and significant ways as new people enter the scene, unaware that they have changed the process. That's why processes should be documented – so they can be followed.
2. Use the process as it is documented; don't avoid it or cut corners. If weaknesses and failures exist, change the process to fix them. Then, document

the new and improved process and use it without exception as the new standard.

3. And as the ranger learned from the angry ranchers, *always* put a name and date on every version of every document, every draft, every revision, and the final version. Name and date. Always.

HOW YOU CAN DO IT TOO

Later in life, I realized that we all have the same opportunity to work **and learn**, consciously watching how things break down, why things get delayed, why and how promises are not kept – with an eye to learning how any process can be improved to mitigate such problems.

—Fechter—

Super-efficient gastronomical delight

THE STORY

For several delightful years, business travel took me every few months to France, for weeks-long trips. My delight was not simply working together with French colleagues. No, the delight was also getting to know them and their culture from regular immersion. And food was part of what I learned.

My French friends would occasionally rib me -- as an American -- when we dined *al fresco* at little French restaurants and watched American tourists walk by. One way to spot American tourists in the crowd is to see who is eating while walking – most often it is an American. That style of eating provides nutrition but misses the mindfulness that comes with dining -- where ambience and environment add to the pleasure of the food tastes, textures, and smells.

The difference between eating while walking versus dining in place was amplified while learning German. *Essen* is a people term and refers to people eating food. *Fressen* is an animal term, referring to animals grazing and eating, often crudely gorging themselves and eating as fast as they can.

Imagine taking your breakfast – *essen* – at the tourist lodge, soaking in the smells of morning coffee, looking out at the clouds and blue sky, and watching the animals in the pastoral scene below, crudely consuming their food – *fressen*.

I look forward to breakfast – not just eating the food, but doing so while reading hard-copy, old-fashioned, paper newspapers and unhurriedly tasting each bite of breakfast.

I wake up early – always too early, but once I'm awake that's it for the day. So, it's time for the wake-up ritual.

I figured out the best of both worlds, a complex and delicious breakfast and eating it with the just-delivered paper newspaper.

Walk into the kitchen, pull up the shades in the dining area. Check outside to see if any deer or pheasants or sandhill cranes are visiting in the wetlands next to our yard. Check blood sugar. Hmmm, good results but

Consuming data in the internet age – are we essen or fressen? ☺

I see a similar comparison – that of reading and thinking [essen] versus bombardment by "breaking news" where tiny, new facts arrive non-stop, their significance not yet understood but moved out of the way as new "breaking news" immediately crowd out the old [fressen].

Internet, radio, and television offer instant news. Kind of like feeling the wind on your face when you step outside. Newspapers summarize those many movements of wind over a day and make sense of trends. Magazines do the same, sensing the wind, but over a month -- so the long-term trends and the meaning of the many data points is easier to see. And books go the next step, collecting and digesting information over a long period of time, so that processes harder to see in real time can be detected and understood.

never quite the desired results. Frown at the results. Put the blood sugar test meter away.

Savor the yellow hues of early sunrise as its colors resonate with the natural beauty and yellowish hues of the wooden cabinets and floor.

Now to breakfast.

Retrieve the bowl I use for cooking oatmeal and flax. Add water to the oatmeal and flax packet in the bowl. Put the bowl into the microwave oven, enter 4:02 on the panel, **but don't yet push START.**

Look out to see if the papers have arrived.

Put a spoon on the counter. And from the drawer above the silverware, take out a cutting board.

Retrieve from the refrigerator the plain yogurt, the jar of pepperoncini, the jar of cocktail onions, and a brown egg. Maybe some radish and some crumbled pretzels. And from the pantry, take the gift from the gods, *a bottle of Tabasco® sauce* (which in our household only lasts 30-days!), and a whole tomato.

Look out to see if the papers have arrived.

The bowl of water, flax, and oatmeal is waiting patiently in the microwave, and the control panel keeps flashing a reminder message, "Push to START".

I retrieve the egg cooker, put it on the counter and plug it in. Measure water to the black line – to cook a perfect soft-boiled egg – one with a runny yolk. Pour the measured water into the egg cooker, puncture the brown egg and put it in the cooker, and add the cooker's top. **Don't yet turn it on!**

Use a special knife to cut up the pepperoncini, the little onions, and the tomato -- a 5-inch knife specially designed to cut tomatoes. With its serrated blade, **it is simply outstanding**. Instead of smashing and mashing what's being cut, it is as precise as a surgical scalpel.

If anyone asks, "What do you want for your birthday... for Christmas...for whatever gift-giving occasion is coming up, your answer is "I want a Wüsthof Classic Tomato Knife." Long into the future, you will smile every time to use that knife.

But I digress...

Breakfast will be a taste delight, but there is something missing from the scene. Right now, it's just food. To cook it and eat it would be like *fressen*. It would not be a dining experience. What's missing? The newspapers.

Look out to see if the papers have arrived.
Yes, they have!

Living in Minnesota means dressing for the weather before going out to the newspaper tubes down the street. With the egg in its cooker, the bowl in the microwave, and the pepperoncini, tomato, and little onions all chopped up and waiting on the cutting board, it's time for the simultaneous plan to spring into action.

Push START on the microwave. The 4:02 timer starts to count down. Switch on the egg cooker. In about seven minutes it will buzz, and the egg will be ready.

With the microwave microwaving and the egg cooker water starting to heat up and turn into steam, I walk over to the closet. I put on the all-weather half-boots, pick a coat, jacket, or sweater that matches the outside weather conditions.

Choose a baseball-style cap to remind me of fun trips to Iceland, Montana, Hawaii, Wisconsin, or …

Make sure the security system is turned off, open the door, and walk, shuffle, or stride (movement style depends on the weather). Walk to the newspaper tube, pick up the *Minneapolis StarTribune*, and unless it is the weekend delivery person who often forgets, also pick up the *New York Times*.

Walk back into the house, return the all-weather boots, coat, and hat back to the closet. Put the newspapers on the table. Take their plastic newspaper-wrappers to the recycle bag and hear the microwave beep to announce that the flax and oatmeal are done.

Remove the cereal bowl from the microwave, add generous shakes of Tabasco® sauce, chopped tomato, onions, and pepperoncini, pretzels, and yogurt. Stir well. Just then the egg cooker buzzes. Remove the egg from its steam bath, saying "Ouch, ouch, ouch…" as it's carried over to running water to cool it off. Peel off the eggshell. Add the egg to the bowl, stir it all together, sit down with the newspapers, and breakfast has started – a **dining experience** of *essen* paced to slowly eating the meal instead of *fressen* to quickly consume the food.

WHAT WAS THE PROCESS OF DISCOVERY?

A lot of words here to explain how to make a breakfast.

But the principle buried in the story was that I've absorbed lean concepts and efficiency tools into my everyday life. The newspapers are a walk away from the house. Getting them before starting breakfast means I'll be tempted to read while trying to make my simple breakfast.

Making breakfast and only going outside for the papers means the cereal is cooling down as I walk out and back in.

Instead, I go for the newspapers during downtime – when the cereal is microwaving, and the egg is in the steam bath.

The key is to be mindful enough to notice the downtime. It didn't take stopwatches and diagrams. All it took was awareness of what I was doing and noticing that a slight change in sequence would enable me to use the cooking time to go for the newspapers. My productivity increased. Not by a huge amount. But at zero cost in time and effort to shuffle the steps as I did.

LESSONS LEARNED:

Step back. When you are "in the process", especially if it repetitious and something you do often. Take some time to appreciate what is happening and then you can have the perspective to work "on the process."

HOW YOU CAN DO IT TOO

Look. Watch. *Notice when you're waiting* for
something before you go on to the next steps. I
always got weather-dressed to walk out for the
newspaper. But I noticed that it took more time to
cook breakfast if I got the newspapers before I
started cooking and stopped preparing to read a bit
here and there.

The cooking cycle itself was just long enough to bring
in the newspapers.

My daily work "in the office" was process
improvement. I carried those principles and tools
into my personal behavior. Not as an obsessive
pattern, just the process of knowing what to look for,
finding examples here and there in daily activities,
and acting on the obvious and easy ones.

—Fechter—

📖 Think of your work as a process

THE STORY

In the early 1990's, I served as a judge in the United States Government's President's Award. The award was presented to Government agencies that had demonstrated the highest level of performance excellence. The criteria included the categories of leadership, strategic planning, customer focus, human resources, information analysis, processes, and results. We performed site visits to evaluate whether or not the agencies applying actually performed up to the levels of excellence that they had stated in their application.

One year, one of the agencies applying for the award was a military base. The base was commanded by a four-star general. He was a handsome man, immaculately groomed with a disciplined military posture. I was the leader of the team assigned to perform the site visit.

The day opened with a 20-minute briefing by the general. He gave an overview of the organization and summarized their achievements. As leader of the team, I was positioned at the point of a V-shaped table. The general stood in front of me and made his presentation in perfect military style. He gestured smoothly with his right hand while his left hand was comfortably behind his back. His right foot was pointed directly at me with his left foot canted at 15 degrees. His presentation went not one second more nor less than 20 minutes.

After his presentation, it was time to proceed with the evaluation of their performance. I had prepared a series of questions designed to verify that the organization actually did what they said they did.

Since I was the leader of the team, I was assigned to evaluate the LEADERSHIP category and that meant interviewing the general. He began by completely dominating the discussion. He was not about to let some Minnesota farm boy get the upper hand. But I was the leader of the team. I was supposed to be leading the discussion not taking the back seat. In my mind, I pondered how I could get control of the meeting. I decided that the only way I could do that would be to ask him a dumb question. He would have to be polite to me because after all I was a member of the team that would decide whether or not they won the President's Award.

The dumb question I ask him was: "General, do you flow chart your daily routine?" He enthusiastically said "OH YES", jumped up from his chair, grabbed a rolled up sheet of paper from the top of a file cabinet, unrolled it, and showed me how he had charted out every detail of his daily routine, starting with brushing his teeth when he got up. So much for dumb questions. He did, in fact, demonstrate outstanding leadership skills.

Looking at the big picture, what we observed at that base was an organization where the leaders had a vision of performance excellence but also paid attention to the details necessary to achieve that vision. Everyone in the organization thought of their work as a process. They had expectations of breakthrough performance and they were able to execute the strategies necessary to achieve that level of performance simply by carrying out the process. Some wise person once said, "Dreams must have both wings and feet." That is what we saw at this base.

WHAT WAS THE PROCESS OF DISCOVERY?

In many organizations, the leaders have a clear vision of what they would like their organization to be, but they are operationally challenged. They simply fail to pay attention to the detail necessary to achieve that vision. Those details are regarded as trivial work that can be delegated to lower levels in the organization. Most of the time it never happens. This is illustrated by a fictional story about a Navy admiral. His strategy for defeating enemy submarines was to boil the oceans. The submarines would have to surface to escape the heat. Then they could easily be picked off by the Navy's destroyers. The captain said, "But Admiral, "How are we going to boil the oceans?" The admiral replied "I'm in charge of strategy. You are in charge of tactics."

My experience at the military base gave me new insights into process management and its importance. They were a vivid example of process management being applied on a daily basis to all of their work. They proved that all work can be defined as a process. Gradually, I came to the realization that that is true.

Yet many organizations do not view their work in the context of a process. As a result, much of the work performed in organizations is random and chaotic. The day-to-day routine is inefficient, and many errors are made. Workers are frustrated because they are blamed for problems that are not their fault. Still, people resist viewing their work as a process because it sounds bureaucratic and it is perceived to inhibit innovation.

Another story illustrates this point. On one occasion, I was invited to advise a consulting company about processes. They insisted that there were no processes in the consulting world. Each client is unique, and their requirements are all different. It was impossible to define processes for the client interface. So, I asked them a few questions:

1. Do you ever discover, after a client meeting, that you forgot to ask them some important questions?
2. Do you ever find that a client meeting ended without a complete understanding of that client's needs?
3. Do you ever find that clients appear to change their minds after you thought you had agreed upon a working arrangement?

They had to answer "Yes" to all of these questions. In the end, they discovered that these were process questions and that there really were processes in consulting work. They got busy and defined the processes by which they reached agreement on client requirements and their working arrangement with them. Later, they acknowledged that they were a much more effective consulting firm once they had learned how to think about processes.

LESSONS LEARNED:

All work can be defined as a process. Processes detail the methods by which work is performed. Processes should be continually improved and made more efficient.

The late quality expert, W. Edwards Deming, said "If you can't describe what you are doing as a process, you don't know what you are doing."

Here is how process improvement works:

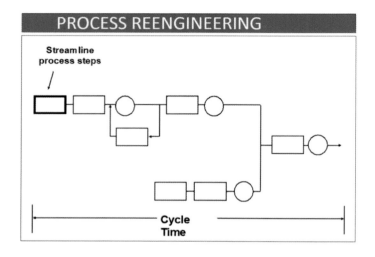

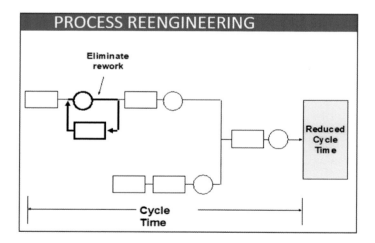

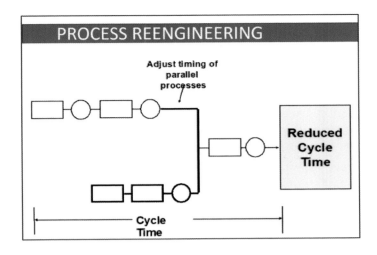

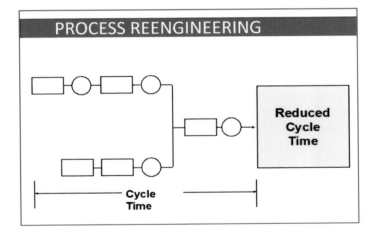

Effective and efficient processes share a common set of characteristics.

- They are DEFINABLE. They specify the basic step-by-step work operations to be performed.
- They are REPEATABLE. Processes are sequences of repeatable activities. They should be communicated, understood, and followed consistently.
- They are PREDICTABLE. Processes should achieve a level of stability that ensures that desired results will be achieved by following steps consistently.

The fundamental purpose of a PROCESS is the preservation of knowledge. The concept of "preservation of knowledge" is important. Once it has been determined "how" work is to be performed, it is important to document the steps (operations) in sufficient detail so that they are performed in the identical way by everyone doing that specific piece of work. Proper definition and documentation are, therefore, very important since they permit the transfer of knowledge to anyone who must perform the work defined in the process. Proper documentation is essential to making the process repeatable.

An actual example helps to illustrate this. A company manufactured very precise, delicate inertial components. A metal block had to move smoothly on a platform as a vehicle accelerated. The product worked exactly as intended until one of the production operators took a week of vacation. Suddenly, nothing worked right. The metal block didn't move at all. When the operator returned from vacation, the production manager asked her how she did it. Nothing worked right while she was gone. She explained that the metal block contained a very small burr. She had to take a fine emery cloth and delicately rub the metal block on it, very lightly because she could not scuff up the block, but just enough to remove the burr. Now everything worked fine again. But none of this was documented in the process instructions. She had discovered this by experience. No one else knew about it. They failed to "preserve the knowledge."

HOW YOU CAN DO IT TOO

Whether you think about it or not, you work in a PROCESS. One is inclined to think of this as bureaucracy. After all, no one likes to look at themselves as robots. People like to believe they need room to be creative and innovative. They do not want to be constrained by having to work within a process. In fact, the exact opposite is true. Well-defined, streamlined processes actually promote creativity. That's because there is no need to waste time redoing work when things go wrong.

So, here is how to proceed:
1. Think through the steps you go through in performing your work.
   a. Do you have the knowledge and resources you need to perform those steps? If not, where and how do you get what is missing?
   b. Are all of the steps necessary?
   c. Could some of the steps be done more efficiently?
2. Think of what operations are performed before the work comes to you
   a. Do you understand what operations are performed before the work gets to you?
   b. Could any of the prior operations be done differently to make your job simpler?
   c. Does any of the work done in prior operations cause you problems?
3. Think of the recipients of your work. Look at them as your customers.
   a. Do your customers understand the work you perform?
   b. Do your customers need all the work you perform? Could some of it be eliminated?
   c. Is some of your work performed just because it is "tradition"?

Speaking about "tradition", there is the story of a cook who always cut off the ends of a roast before he put it in the pan. When asked why he did that, he replied "My mother always did that." When they asked the mother why she did that, she said "Well the pan I had was too small to fit the whole roast in, so I had to cut off the ends." It pays to question things.

From a "big picture" point of view, think of the things that frustrate you in your job. Look at the things that impact your job to see if those frustrations could be eliminated. And, in general, think of ways that the process could be improved.

—Weimerskirch—

Chapter 04
Communicating Effectively

Active listening

THE STORY

Honeywell sent me to many interesting seminars over the course of my career. One of the most valuable ones was the one on active listening. The concept was that total communication between two people can't happen until they are willing to listen deeply to the other person and understand that person's true feelings and viewpoints.

The seminar leader was very effective. There were 15 of us in the seminar. He placed us in chairs in a large circle around the room. He sat in a roller chair in the middle of the room. Then he played the role of a man who was having difficulties in his marriage. He rolled his chair around to each one of us in turn. We were to listen intently to what he said and have empathy with him as he dealt with his assumed troubles.

When he came to me, he was explaining his pain. I said, "Well here is what I would recommend." "NO!!" he said forcefully. You are supposed to listen to me, not give me advice. There were two other vice presidents in the room who also tried to give him advice rather than listen to him. There is probably a message in there somewhere. We are trained to fix problems, not just listen to them.

WHAT WAS THE PROCESS OF DISCOVERY?

It was difficult to learn the concept of active
listening. Throughout our early years, we are taught
to express ourselves. We are taught that we should
have opinions and convince other people of the value
of those opinions. We are not taught to listen. As a
matter of fact, people who don't talk much are
commonly regarded as timid and introverted.

It is possible to be successful by being a good listener.
Calvin Coolidge, our 30th president, was known as
"Silent Cal." A couple of his quotes are interesting.

Calvin Coolidge
Source: Commons.wikimedia.org

We should probably pay attention to the old saying:

> *God gave us two ears and one mouth.*
> *We should listen twice as much as we talk.*

LESSONS LEARNED:

Individuals and organizations should learn and practice the art of active listening. It makes communications more effective and enables deeper understanding of the other person's viewpoints and objectives.

Most organizations that fail or underperform, do so not because they lack the answers. It is because they don't know the questions to ask. In too many Board Rooms, a meeting consists of a series of "talking heads" who make presentations on a variety of topics relating to their expertise. Board members move on to the next topic without discussion of the topic presented. There is no processing of the information and there is no action plan to implement good ideas. Board members nod in agreement and then adjourn the meeting.

Organizational leaders need to actively listen to each other's viewpoints and reach a consensus agreement. Then they need to set an action plan to make the necessary improvements.

HOW YOU CAN DO IT TOO

The same concept of active listening can be practiced at the individual level as well as the organizational level. In interpersonal communication, too many people believe that persuasion is a matter of being highly articulate. They try to win their point by out-talking the other person. They do not listen while the other person is talking. Their mind is on the next point they intend to make.

The concept of active listening, on the other hand, is based on the premise that communication is more effective if one listens to the viewpoint of the other person. Salesmanship is more effective when one can show how his or her product or service can meet the other persons requirements and expectations.

—Weimerskirch—

Ask more questions

THE STORY

Back in the 1990s, my company, Bull HN
Information Systems, moved its headquarters from
Minneapolis, Minnesota, to Boston, Massachusetts.
Bull HN had originally been **H**oneywell Information
Systems, with partnership and owner relationships
with Bull Computer out of France and **N**EC out of
Japan. The new company – Bull HN – was split from
Honeywell, Inc. which at that time was
headquartered in Minneapolis.

As with most company mergers, acquisitions, and
divestitures, it was a time of a thousand questions.
Some technical. Some policy. Some logistical. Some
personal. And so on. And with all the questions came
many answers. Some precise. Some vague. Some
wrong. Some that raised even more questions. And so
on.

The answers I heard to my questions bring back that
famous observation: "**I know you think you
understand what you thought I said, but I'm not sure
you realize that what you heard is not what I
meant.**"

The move date from Minneapolis was accelerated, so
senior executives and managers had to commute to
Boston, Phoenix, Paris, and Milan over the next
several months, to be on-site at locations where
regular and transition activities were underway.

Personal decisions flooded into the day for everyone
making the move – decisions about selling and
buying houses, investigating options in Boston and
making arrangements for children and schools, new
doctors, new dentists, new mechanics to maintain
and fix our cars. These kinds of conversations slipped

in between conversations about company logistics, about replacing personnel who chose not to move, about finding and moving into new offices, and more.

Because we had nearly six months to complete the transition, people could scout out areas around Boston to be more informed about the positive and negative things associated with each locale.

> *"I know that you believe you understand what you think I said, but I'm not sure you realize that what you heard is not what I meant"*
>
> Attributed to Greenspan during a Capitol Hill hearing.
>
> However, the earliest known print attribution is to Robert McCloskey, U.S. State Department spokesman, by Marvin Kalb, CBS reporter, in a 1984 *TV Guide*, citing an unspecified press briefing during the Vietnam war.
> https://en.wikiquote.org/wiki/Alan_Greenspan

In my case, shortly after I had signed papers to have a new home built in Minnesota, rumors of a move to Boston had started to circulate. I needed to know dates and plans about the headquarters relocation so that I could make yes/no decisions about going ahead with the new house. Some rumors said that only certain functions were relocating and that other functions would remain in the Twin Cities.

How could I know whether I was moving or staying? My function in worldwide quality improvement was implemented at all locations, wherever the company had operations; I could travel to field sites around the world and then return to my base wherever it was – whether it be in Minneapolis, Boston, or elsewhere.

So, to clear up rumors about who was moving to Boston and who was staying in the Twin Cities, I asked my boss, who was head of operations for the company. "I've heard the rumors that we are **all** moving to Boston. Are they true?"

He laughed, put his head back, and said with a chuckle. "I'm not moving to Boston!" We both laughed. He was truly a great team leader; I consider it a privilege to have worked for and with him.

And as high-level managers often do, he would sometimes say "I" when referring to Operations and its thousands of personnel, not always using "I" to mean just himself in the singular.

For example, "I'm going to implement the new design documentation system" when referring to plans within operations, but not referring to specific steps that he personally, himself, would be taking about the new design documentation system.

In answering my question, he said: "*I'm* not moving to Boston."

But *what I heard* was, "The rumors are not true. We are not moving to Boston."

"I know you think you understand what you thought I said, but I'm not sure you realize that what you heard is not what I meant."

About a month after the construction started on my new house in Minnesota, we were all informed that indeed, all Honeywell Information Systems management positions in Minneapolis were moving to Boston. I was moving to Boston.

We owned that new house in Minnesota for 13 months; I only lived in it for three months and spent the rest of those 13 months living in a rental apartment in Boston, or working in Paris, Phoenix, Milan, and elsewhere.

He had answered my question with, "I'm not moving to Boston." But what I heard was, "The rumors are not true. We are not moving to Boston."

He did commute for many months and then retired in Minnesota; He never did relocate his home to Boston. What I should have asked is "Boss, will *I* be relocating to Boston after the new company is formed?"

Once I knew for certain that I was relocating, I spent non-work hours in Boston scouting for the best place to live. Traffic was notoriously bad throughout the area, so the wrong choice about *where you lived versus where you worked* could mean no big deal or could mean many hours each day creeping slowly or dead-stopped waiting for *"something ahead in traffic"* to clear up.

Our offices were in Billerica, in the northwest part of the Boston metro area. My new boss in Boston (after my Minnesota boss retired) lived in Newton, in the southwest part of the metro area. So, before we picked our home's location, I asked him about commuting. "How much time does it take you to drive to and from Newton?" He thought about it and replied that in his experience there were seldom any commuting problems from his home to work and that it wasn't really that much of an issue.

In fact, he noted that he normally drove right at the speed limit both ways when commuting.
Only after I moved to Westford, Massachusetts, northwest of Billerica, did I realize that while I'd asked if he had any *best home location suggestions* to avoid commuting hassles, what I heard in his answer

was that commuting issues were overblown and that
I need not be concerned.

What I didn't know, when I asked about commuting,
was that he left for work very, very early, about 5
a.m., and left from work to return home very late,
about 8 p.m. or later.

The reason he had no issues with commuting was
because he left home before the rush hour started
and returned home after the rush hour was over.

Commuting was indeed an issue for me. And while I
was generally OK with commuting times, I was often
frustrated that my 15-mile drive down Highway 3
could take 15-minutes to three-hours, depending on
"something" ahead.

WHAT WAS THE PROCESS OF DISCOVERY?

We all do a bit of selective listening, often hearing
what we want to hear, but not always receiving a
complete and accurate answer to our internal
questions. An assertive feedback technique is most
helpful to avoid surprises.

For example, I'd asked my boss if we were moving to
Boston. He'd replied, "I'm not moving to Boston." I
interpreted that to mean that I wasn't moving to
Boston.

What I should have done after his reply was to use
an assertive response. Something like, "So, myself
and the rest of your executive team are not moving to
Boston. Right?" He would have chuckled and
answered, "Well, you are on my team and my team is
moving."

And when I asked my new boss in Boston about best
home locations to avoid commuting hassles, I should
have followed up on his answer by an assertive

follow-up. Something like, "Boston is famous for traffic delays at rush hour. Where are the best neighborhoods for me to find a house – so I can avoid traffic delays at rush hour?"

LESSONS LEARNED:

1. People hear first what they want to hear, and any ambiguity that confirms their wishes or hopes or that allays their concern is the message they want to hear.
2. Murphy's Law states that anything that can go wrong, will go wrong. Perhaps Murphy's cousin used another saying, "Whatever can be misunderstood will be misunderstood."
3. As the saying goes, if you assume but don't say the assumptions out loud, you risk making an **ASS** out of **U** and **ME**.

HOW YOU CAN DO IT TOO

1. Don't phrase questions as implied but unstated Yes/No confirmations of your assumptions. Think literally when you form the question. Hold your tongue -- until you've decided whether you should include questions about assumptions, not just a Yes/No verification of your unspoken assumptions.

   When you talk, listen to yourself, *but not only as yourself.*

   Rather, listen as if you were a peer hearing it, as if you were a customer hearing it, as if you were a job candidate hearing it, etc.

2. An effective technique is to ask listeners to tell you what they heard. If he had asked me to confirm what he told me, I'd have said, "I'm

not moving to Boston. I can go ahead with my new house in Minnesota." He would have chuckled, and said, "Not quite."

"I know you think you understand what you thought I said, but I'm not sure you realize that what you heard is not what I meant."

—Fechter—

📖 Don't surprise me in front of my boss

THE STORY

An exciting milestone.

Our executives recognized that customer expectations had moved beyond banking basics of having a safe place to store monies, providing checking accounts, and offering loans. Those were still key expectations, but in addition, people expected 24/7 access to services through ATMs, a wider variety of investment funds, easy access to facilities and bank personnel, service levels that left competitors in the dust, and more...

Customer satisfaction was acknowledged as critically important, but with a series of branch and bank acquisitions, personnel turnover, and changing customer expectations, available measures of customer satisfaction were incomplete, difficult to aggregate and compare, and not yet well integrated with performance goals.

We needed a comprehensive set of measures that would allow management to better understand:
- what delighted customers,
- what infuriated them,
- what frustrated them,
- and what motivated them to select our bank and not a competitor.

Getting better data was a business investment. First, to ensure that we knew what customers expected – traditional and new expectations. And second, to establish a timely, solid, and up-to-date system to measure customer satisfaction. Gaps would become known -- between what customers expected and what they experienced, and we would know what needed fixing.

Fix and prevent those gaps and business would grow; customer defection would be diminished.

A renowned survey firm was engaged. Endorsement and support for regular surveys was secured from the bank's nation-wide geography and at key, management levels. We were off to get the metrics!

Some field problems delayed the planned completion date. We had intended to have results at the beginning of the next quarter. That way, they could be shared at the senior level and corrective action could then be cascaded throughout the bank organization and its nation-wide, geographic locations.

Action plans to close gaps would be initiated, performance goals would be more tightly aligned with customer satisfaction metrics, and we'd see the positive effects of improvements in the next survey.

In face-to-face and group meetings, I saw support and interest growing. Bankers love numbers and data as the basis for action, and we would soon have those numbers.

Finally, the delays were over, and the survey results were in.

But, because of the field delay, and with the top-level, quarterly operations meeting only a day or two away, our department was rushed. We studied the report and looked at satisfaction levels, trends, comparisons by state, by service types, and many other analyses. I had a timeslot reserved on the operations agenda and we had no time to do much more than analyze and prepare our report for the operations meeting with the C-suite of executives covering customer-facing departments and infrastructure departments within the bank.

The survey was fruitful. Some performance levels were outstanding, some average... good results, some issues, and a lot of opportunities to close gaps and remove things that were causing customer dissatisfaction. This was statistically valid, actionable data!

My time arrived on the agenda. With great enthusiasm I started to go through the results. I was thrilled that we now had the customer satisfaction data they'd been waiting for — data that would prioritize where the problems were, and which gaps were most important to our customers and where improvements were needed.

However, things started to turn dark. No one except our department had seen the data, the analyses, the trends, or the comparisons. Lots of good results but customers also named things they were unhappy with.

As opportunity gaps here and there were displayed, the CEO's head turned with unhappiness to specific executives in charge. Call center, why weren't these problems fixed? Dissatisfaction with check processing times. Why? And so on. Other executives frowned as their function's satisfaction data came up and the CEO turned to each of them asking why those just-reported problems hadn't yet been addressed.

The reason? Prior to doing the expanded survey we had never before had these comprehensive results. Traditional metrics hadn't included many aspects that were now important to customers.

But I had unintentionally created a crisis.

Most executives had inadequate answers to the CEO because in this operations meeting they were seeing the results for the first time, just as the CEO was seeing them for the first time.

We had initially lost schedule time due to field problems before the survey could be started. But once the data arrived, we had been so enthusiastic to analyze the results and prepare our presentation that we had not included time to brief process and product executives in advance of the operations meeting. This was a new set of metrics and much more thorough and detailed than what had been available in the past. I'd blindsided multiple execs.

WHAT WAS THE PROCESS OF DISCOVERY?

We lived through my error, but it was painful and unnecessarily stressful.

The executives and the CEO accepted the valuable information from our customers and the execs acted on the facts and subsequently improved many areas of their responsibility.

But I had to rebuild trust and communications with all of the executives.

Before my presentation was finished, with all those useful but *sprung-by-surprise* customer survey results, I turned off the projector, paused for a short but felt-like-forever pause, and then said aloud, *"I'm sorry. I made a major mistake. In my enthusiasm to share some really good findings and some things customers really aren't happy with, I unintentionally put all of you on the spot. You are **my** customers. I'm going to fix my process to better support and inform you in the future."*

They were gracious, discussed some major action items, and the meeting moved to the next agenda item. I survived; customer satisfaction data and improvement plans were on the agenda for future, quarterly, operations meetings. And prior to those operations meetings I had a bevy of scheduled, pre-meeting briefings to share data and analyses with process owners – before the operations reviews.

LESSONS LEARNED:

My lifelong lesson: **Don't Surprise Me in Front of My Boss.** If you learn something important that is beyond your own responsibilities, share the information in a timely manner with others who own the process. Those people are key stakeholders and the odds that they will help improve things are much increased the sooner they hear that their corrective action is needed.

HOW YOU CAN DO IT TOO

When you make a mistake, admit it. Acknowledge the negative consequences of the mistake. Highlight how it happened, *and how the PROCESS that was used will be changed.*

> Admitting You Were Wrong Doesn't Make You Weak -- It Makes You Awesome!
> Amy Rees Anderson, *FORBES*, 01 May 2013

—Fechter—

Everyday outstanding flight attendant

THE STORY

I haven't met another like her, and I still miss her.

For several years we lived in Westford, Massachusetts and I travelled frequently to company sites throughout the USA and overseas. It was nearly equidistant in miles to drive from my Westford home to Boston's Logan Airport as to drive north to Manchester, New Hampshire and take a commuter flight to Logan – thereby missing the high-density traffic and congested tunnels in Boston.

On one of those Manchester to Boston flights, our commuter plane was filled to the gills. Not enough room in the overhead tray to stow coats and other things, so we were holding our coats and our feet were resting upon the carry-on materials we were able to bring aboard; most other carry-ons had to be checked before boarding.

In this cramped environment, people were grumpy and frustrated.

The door closed. Then, from her spot in the back of the plane, the unseen flight attendant started her microphone-assisted announcement about all the safety things, seat belts, oxygen masks, water landing, and such. Almost immediately the grumpy passengers relaxed and turned into attentive, happy guests.

Why?
Unlike most safety communications and announcements that are often read aloud as fast as humanly possible – *perhaps flight attendants receive a bonus if they can get through the entire*

announcement in less than 60-seconds? – unlike that, she was "talking – as if to *each* of us, personally".

Her pace and delivery were at human conversational speed. She was happy. She shared it. She started with this warm and bubbly greeting...

"Hello... <pause> ...

we are happy that <pause>

you <slight pause>

chose <slight pause>

us <pause>

to fly *you* safely and quickly to Boston's Logan airport."

Passengers put down their things, stopped what they were doing, and listened to her.

Try it yourself. Say aloud, with grace, and like a conversation you're having with a best friend, "Hello... <pause> ... we are happy that <pause> *you* <slight pause> *chose* <slight pause> us <pause> to fly *you* safely and quickly to Boston's Logan airport."

She was truly communicating with each of us. Not simply as a checklist announcement that must be completed before takeoff. No. It was a conversation like she was making eye contact with each of us individually as she spoke – even though she was in the rear of the plane and none could see her without turning around.

When she finished the announcement, passengers were all smiles. She walked forward to the front of the plane, then slowly walked back, checking that each passenger's seat belt was fastened. Smiling and making eye contact with each person as she passed by.

More than a few passengers said to her, "That was great!", or "Thank you, that was nice."

We'd been transformed from a bunch of hurried, grumpy, uncomfortable people into a friendly group of friendly people off on a very routine but suddenly delightful trip to Logan Airport.

These were true in the 1930s and are still true in the 2020s.

<u>Six Ways to Make People Like You</u>

1: Become genuinely interested in other people.
2: Smile.
3: Remember that a person's name is to him or her the sweetest and most important sound...
4: Be a good listener. Encourage others to talk about themselves.
5: Talk in terms of the other person's interests.
6: Make the other person feel important -- and do it sincerely.

From "How to Win Friends and Influence People", by Dale Carnegie, 1936

WHAT WAS THE PROCESS OF DISCOVERY?

She'd used the same words as any other flight attendant reading the same script. But she made us feel that she cared about us listening to her, and that it wasn't just a task; it was setting the stage for a good flight.

I don't know her name. I don't think we even noticed her looks, except the eye contact and the smile.

What I remember was that she made us feel that we were in her care and that she cared how we felt about it. And her subsequent eye contact was person-to-person.

To this day -- with over 45 years of flying and almost two million passenger miles under my seat belt -- when they make the safety announcement – as quickly and as monotone as humanly possible –I remember her, I smile, and I miss her.

LESSONS LEARNED:

Much of our day-to-day social interaction is done by habit.

The doctor asks, "How are you?" and you reply, "Fine." But the doctor seldom follows-up with, "Then why you are here if you are fine?"

Most of us go through three phases when learning a new skill such as making a speech. The first time through the material we focus on staying within the time limits, fitting everything in. The second time we focus on delivery, staying within the time limits but incorporating refinements like pauses and emphasizing highlights. And for the third and subsequent tellings, we focus on the message.

My outstanding flight attendant was well into the third phase, covering all the required content but aiming to communicate, not just say the words in the script.

HOW YOU CAN DO IT TOO

Treat every human interaction as an opportunity; over time this can become your everyday style, not a forced or unnatural way of behaving.

Set the stage – stop looking at the screen, put down the phone, close the book, and put down the pen. Think about whether your body language matches what you are saying aloud.

Pay attention. Take more time. Listen to their input – summarize what they said.

Do not develop your response while they speak.

The good news? These techniques work.

The bad news? So few people do them well that when we experience well-done interactions, we take special notice, and we are delighted.

In Minneapolis, a wonderful, caring woman named Mary Jo Copeland, founded *Sharing and Caring Hands* in 1984. She personally spoke at our church at about the same time she founded *Sharing and Caring Hands.*

She is known throughout the Twin Cities for her work, has met Pope Francis and received the Presidential Citizens Medal in 2013.

With Mary Jo, everything is personal, and all relationships are real, not fake.

A quote she often cites with a smile, when asking for donations and volunteers, is from Dr. Seuss, "To the world you may be one person; but to one person you may be the world."

—Fechter—

OK, but will it hurt?

THE STORY

This Photo by Unknown Author is licensed under CC BY-SA

Dr. Caroline McGill is a legend.

She was Montana's first pathologist, having earned the first doctoral degree granted to a woman at the University of Missouri. Later, she graduated from Johns Hopkins Medical School with the highest grades in her class, worked for a time with the Mayo brothers in Rochester, Minnesota at the Mayo Clinic, and then opened a medical clinic in Butte, Montana.

She is a legend to Montanans, but to my father – when he was a toddler -- she was the lady who regularly stopped over for coffee and

---

Created a legacy

Montana State University School of Nursing would probably not exist -- had it not been for Dr. Caroline McGill.

Likewise, when she founded the world-renowned **Museum of the Rockies** in Bozeman, Montana in 1957. Thousands of pioneer relics – tools, pictures, diaries, and more would have been tossed as people moved on, moved away, or moved up. She was instrumental in saving such relics and the records that explained their significance and provenance.

A woman of many firsts, she was already a practicing pathologist – Montana's first – when she returned to school to receive her MD. She graduated first in her class at Johns Hopkins University Medical School, but she was not permitted to attend graduation because she had completed medical school in two years instead of four. She remembered that slight throughout her career.

breakfast on her way to, or from, a long day or night at the hospital and clinic.

This is the story as my father related it to me, about a memorable event with Dr. McGill when he was about four or five years old.

One morning, as his mother and Dr. McGill talked at the kitchen table over coffee and breakfast, Dr. McGill stopped talking and started watching my father, John, as he walked around the kitchen. She mentioned something quietly to John's mother. They both stopped talking and quietly studied his movements. Back and forth. Happy and content. Back and forth, but never quite standing fully erect as he walked around the kitchen.

Again, they commented quietly to each other. And watched.

Then, Dr. McGill made her pronouncement, "Yes, I think we need to cut off his feet."

He stopped walking and looked at them both. She was such a good friend to his mother. She was a nice lady who had always been kind to him. Now ·· she proposed to cut off his feet?

He recalled being quickly swooped up to stand on the kitchen counter. Analyzing his feet ever more closely as he stood there. Dr. McGill said again, "Yes, we need to cut off his feet."

He tried to act as brave as a four or five-year-old could act and asked in a tiny voice, "Will it hurt?" "No, you'll hardly notice it!" was Dr. McGill's quick and hearty reply.

His mother found the scissors and handed them to Dr. McGill, who then carefully and swiftly cut the feet from the bottom of his footed pajamas!

He had grown, and his mother hadn't noticed that the footed pajamas had become too short; he couldn't stand completely erect. That morning, Dr. McGill had watched him walk with a hunched back and knew that she needed to cut the feet off of his one-piece pajama outfit.

After his one-piece pajamas were footless, he could stand up straight.

At that point, his tears changed to a big smile. He told them that he thought Dr. McGill meant she was going to cut the feet from his body...and that was why he was so timid and afraid.

Much laughter, big hugs all around, and much more laughter by all.

A lesson for us all as we communicate?

WHAT WAS THE PROCESS OF DISCOVERY?

Two of the most important authority figures in toddler John's life had announced, "Yes, we need to cut off his feet." He was smart, and he understood every word. He didn't understand why they wanted to do it, but he felt too intimidated to ask. His mother cared for him every day. And Dr, McGill was not only the family doctor but was also a daily friend and visitor to their home.

He understood the words and interpreted them to mean a frightening thought -- that he would lose his feet.

To John, feet meant feet.

His feet.

To Dr. McGill and John's mother, feet meant the lower part of his one-piece pajamas. Dr. McGill and

John's mother were having a happy thought that he would be more comfortable after the pajama feet were removed. His unhappy thought was fear.

LESSONS LEARNED:

1. It takes two to communicate. The message one person sends is not necessarily the same message that is received by the other person.

This sidebar sounds like a comedy routine but was a real conversation between my wife's mother and her sister.

Context: one sister's parakeet had died. Separately, the other sister had heard that a neighbor up the street had passed away.

One sister asked, *"Where is he going to be buried?"*
..."In the back yard"
"What! You can't bury him in the back yard! That's wrong and probably illegal."
..."No, it isn't. People do it all the time."
"Are you crazy? They do not."

Then the first sister said, "He's just a parakeet. We can bury him in the back yard."

And the other sister, now convulsed in laughter, said, *"Oh! I thought you were talking about your neighbor who just died!"*

---

2. The words or facts may be transmitted and received with 100% accuracy, but the meaning of the sent message may not be the same when interpreted by the receiver.

3. People perceive things through the filter of their own beliefs, emotions, and knowledge. Even though you are transmitting properly doesn't mean that the other person will receive the message you intend to send.

> A friend's personal experience:
> *On a sunny Florida morning he was out for his morning walk. Along the way he met one of his neighbors, a teacher, who was also out in the morning sunshine walking her dog.*
>
> *In an innocent bit of banter, and meaning to be friendly he said with a smile," Oh, another day off?"*
>
> *Her response – body language and words -- was frustrated, deflated, and defeated. She responded to his cheery, "Oh, another day off?" with her "Awwww, **come on! Really??**"*
>
> *His comment may not have been the most brilliant version of a morning "Hello," but it was meant as an innocent, friendly comment.*
>
> *Turns out that she was very sensitive to the fact that many people think teachers get too many days off. So, she took offence.*
>
> *She heard clearly what he said. But her interpretation of the message was far, far away from his intent.*

HOW YOU CAN DO IT TOO

Be sensitive to how other people are receiving your message. Consider their body language and facial emotions – if it seems at odds with what you expected. And be prepared to check with them about what they heard, so you can correct the message if it was not received as you intended.

Define your terms.

- When people hear your words, take time to define.
- **"Our company is moving…"** can be words of doom if personnel think their unit is **being relocated.** They may stop listening because they are afraid.
- Or, those same words can be motivating if personnel understand that the company, or its products, or its strategy is **moving forward.** They are listening with enthusiasm for more detail.

Be specific. *Better. Improved. Leader.* ← *Those are general adjectives.* Be specific -- say what is expected, by when, and how we will know it really happened. For example, within 20 months after the project, yield will improve by 22%.

Use pronouns with utmost caution. For example, "*They* have had problems with their personnel and customers. *Their friends* reported the issues. *They* were terrible." Who had problems? Were the issues terrible? Or were the friends terrible?

In general, to ensure that your messages are getting through as you intended, ask listeners to tell you in their own words what they heard.
"You're going to cut the feet off of my body?"

Photo by John Fechter

—Fechter—

📖 Rank has its privileges – or not

THE STORY

When I was Chairman of the Judges Panel for the Malcolm Baldrige National Quality Award, I made a business trip to Australia. After some daytime meetings, I was invited to a dinner with the regional managers of many of the large companies in the Pacific Rim area. The Pacific Rim includes all the countries that border the Pacific Ocean and extends down to Australia and New Zealand. These were subsidiaries of large United States companies operating in that region. Since I was from the United States and was Chairman of the Judges Panel, I was the honored guest.

During the course of our discussions that evening, I was asked questions like:
- What did I think was the future of Ford Motor Company?
- What did I see as the economic outlook for the Pacific Rim Region?

The fact of the matter was that I really knew nothing about those topics. But since I was a presumed expert, I felt obliged to answer. I didn't think I could sit there and say, "I don't know." I couldn't tell how much stock they put in my comments, but it was probably more than they should have.

This story illustrates that people tend to equate credibility with rank. It's a false pretense.

I can recall other examples of this misconception:
- I was serving as a consultant to an organization that was applying for the Malcolm Baldrige National Quality Award. I

was asked to review the application with one of the organization's vice presidents. She looked at the application and then said, "The criteria ask the wrong questions." Now the Baldrige criteria has been developed by thousands of hours of work by hundreds of the country's best experts on the topic. Yet, this vice president felt comfortable saying that it was all wrong and that she knew better simply because she was a vice president.

-A four-star general wrote a book on quality. The general's knowledge of quality was shallow at best, but the book was regarded as credible simply because he was a four-star general.

-Numerous meetings where people look to the ranking member to have all the answers and are reluctant to make their own informed input simply because they are outranked.

WHAT WAS THE PROCESS OF DISCOVERY?

At Honeywell, we had a workshop designed to get the greatest benefit from people's knowledge. In the workshop exercise, our airplane crashes in a hot dessert. Everyone survives with no injuries. However, our radio is broken, and we have no contact with the outside world – this was before cell phones. We have salvaged a few miscellaneous items including a bottle of brandy and a piece of aluminum. The object is to figure out how we can survive until outside help can discover us and rescue us.

In the exercise, we are each asked to devise a survival plan in private without talking to any of our teammates. After we have developed our individual plans, we met as a team to develop a team plan. The idea is that the team plan should pool our collective knowledge and be better than any of the individual plans.

On our team, there was a man who had had survival training. He knew how he would use each of the miscellaneous items to survive until help could get to us. However, he was a very quiet man, reluctant to speak up. The rest of us did not realize that he was an expert on the topic, and we did not take his knowledge into account. As a result, his individual plan was vastly superior to our team plan.

That workshop was the first time I had heard the word "synergy." The Merriam Webster dictionary defines synergy as:
> *Synergy is the benefit that results when two or more agents work together to achieve something either one couldn't have achieved on its own. It's the concept of the whole being greater than the sum of its parts.*

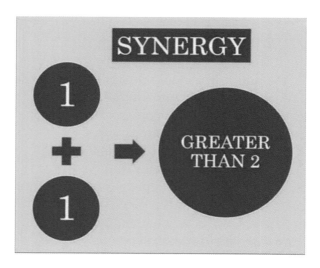

We had failed to achieve synergy in the workshop, but we came to appreciate the power of it.

LESSONS LEARNED:

People assume competence based on a person's status whether that competence is real or not. This tendency inhibits communications and fails to take advantage of all the knowledge present. Synergy is a very important concept. In any group meeting, every individual has a piece of the information that is valuable to achieve the group's objective.

Yet, in most meetings, we defer to the most senior person whether they have the appropriate information or not. People like to hear themselves talk. Very few engage in active listening. Little attempt is made to take advantage of all the information available in the room. Few meetings achieve synergy.

HOW YOU CAN DO IT TOO

Don't be too impressed with people's rank. They may have special knowledge in some areas, but it may not be relevant to the current situation. Make them demonstrate their knowledge of the topic at hand.

When you are in meetings, try to take advantage of all the knowledge in the room. Pay attention to those individuals who appear to have information relevant to the situation. Then try to get them to speak up. Be an active listener. Be conscious of situations where people try to take advantage of their rank. On the other hand, take advantage of their rank if that helps you persuade others to your point of view.

—Weimerskirch—

Chapter 05
Accepting Responsibility

Big or small, do it right or not at all

THE STORY

Do It Right. And That's All 😊

She was just out of high school, with excellent typing and organizing skills, but no job experience yet. During the job interview, I asked about her perspective on quality; our department was focused on improving supplier quality. She perked up with a big smile, "I believe what my father always said, a senior manager in Minneapolis. *"Big or small, do it right or not at all."*

We hired her, and she was a thorough, conscientious, and enthusiastic new member of our team. Her work was flawless and on-time. And her can-do personality was frosting on the cake. Everyone liked working with her on their projects.

One day, she put a folder on my desk that contained many rough notes from our group's working session the day before -- calendar dates scribbled on Post-It® notes, some charts, some graphs, and highlight notes from participants about Who, What, and When action items.

It was all there, but incomprehensible in its raw form.

I picked up the folder from my desk and opened it, expecting to see everything neatly organized into a *Summary* of the event and its conclusions, then the *Actions* and who was responsible for each, with those dates included in the master schedule. Finally, there was to be a *Background* section with content from the raw Post-It® notes, flip chart scribbles, and other handwritten highlights translated into clearly typed text.

But – the folder she dropped on my desk was exactly as I had handed it to her – unchanged, with the same rough notes, scribbles, Post-It® notes, charts and graphs from the working session. They had not been organized, had not been typed-up, and had not been formatted into *Summary*, *Actions*, and *Background* sections for the team to review and use as their To-Do list for follow-through.

I asked her to come into my office. Her smile brightened the room, she sat down with her note pad, and said "What's up?"

I showed her the folder. I showed that the materials hadn't been organized and were not yet ready for distribution to the project team. With a smile, she agreed.

I was puzzled. Before this, she had done excellent work on every task and project. But this particular task was unfinished – not even started, and she was acknowledging that fact with a smile.

She said, "I looked at the mess and saw how much work it was going to be. And because I don't know that project very well yet, I wasn't sure that I could get it all put together correctly." And with a friendly smile, she added, "So, I remembered the job interview when I said for quality, 'Do it right, or not at all.' And because I wasn't sure I could do it right, I didn't do it at all."

Silence. More silence. Awkward silence.

Then, with some humorous banter, I explained that organizing such a mess of notes was a major part of her job. We talked about how she could fill in missing or incomplete details through questions and 1:1

discussions with project team members. Having done that, she would be able to produce the summary document.

She was very sincere, and said, "Oh."

Awkward silence. Then with enthusiasm and a smile she stood up, took the folder, and said, "OK, I'll go get it done!"

She left the office and did a very professional job, filling in details and clarifying incomplete or uncertain items with help from team members. The team accepted her summary and used it as a roadmap to complete their To-Do's -- on schedule.

And during the entire time we worked together, she continued to do excellent work on every task and project. As time went by, when we discussed similar assignments and projects she needed to do, she would have a quick smile and a comment, **"Do it right. And that's all."**

WHAT WAS THE PROCESS OF DISCOVERY?

This was a valuable learning experience for me.
I learned lessons about
- clear communication of expectations,
- about empowering team members,
- and about how powerfully positive it can be to objectively critique "what went wrong with the process" without criticizing or blaming the person.

Our team's approach to confront defects was always: 1) If results are not what we want. 2) What needs to be changed to get the results we want?

If incoming parts were out of specification, we detailed how many parts, how often, how much, etc. We shared such detail with suppliers and reviewed whether they had the correct drawings, whether their production process was staying within specifications, whether the damage happened in shipping, etc.
With the focus on facts and not blame, we had enthusiastic cooperation to find problems, figure out the causes, and then work together to change the process and fix it.

For more on this topic of continuous improvement of all processes I recommend that you read the excellent book, _**PRINCIPLES**_, by Ray Dalio, 2017.

LESSONS LEARNED:

Ensure clear communication of expectations: When receiving an assignment, say it back in your own words. That's *measuring twice* to confirm what you're being asked to do.

To optimize performance, coach, don't blame.

iMPROVE!

Empower people: To be empowered means that a person has the means to deliver what their customers or clients expect from them.

Objectively critique performance – critique the process in use -- without criticizing or blaming the person: Confront the facts without maligning the intentions or competency of people using processes that may not working correctly.

HOW YOU CAN DO IT TOO

She stopped the process because she wasn't empowered; she lacked needed detail and couldn't proceed. After our conversation, she realized that just stopping the process wasn't enough. She also had to ask for missing details so she would be empowered to do what we'd asked of her.

"Do it right, and that's all." If I lack the means to do it right, raise my hand and ask for help. And management, 1) thank people who raise their hand

and "measure twice before cutting once", and 2) go empower them with what they need.

__There is an old adage that applies to every task we're asked to do:__

"Measure twice and cut once." That's obvious if you're cutting lumber. And like the carpenter who is asked to "cut all the wood into two-foot lengths", and verifies by asking, "cut **all** of the 2x4's and **all** of the 4ft x 8ft plywood sheets into two-foot lengths?" The requestor would probably change the request to "cut **all the 2x4's** into two-foot lengths."

By NASA/JPL/Corby Waste -
http://www.vitalstatistics.info/uploads/mars%20climate%20orbiter.jp
g (see also http://www.jpl.nasa.gov/pictures/solar/mcoartist.html),
Public Domain,
https://commons.wikimedia.org/w/index.php?curid=390903

A high-tech example:
The Mars Climate Orbiter ... a 638-kilogram (1,407 lb) robotic space probe launched by NASA on December 11, 1998 to study the Martian climate, Martian atmosphere, and surface changes and to act as the communications relay in the Mars Surveyor '98 program for Mars Polar Lander.

However, on September 23, 1999, communication with **the spacecraft was lost as the spacecraft went into orbital insertion, due to ground-based computer software which produced output in non-SI units of pound-force seconds (lbf·s) instead of the SI units of newton-seconds (N·s) specified in the contract between NASA and Lockheed.** The spacecraft encountered Mars on a trajectory that brought it too close to the planet, and it was either destroyed in the atmosphere or re-entered heliocentric space after leaving Mars' atmosphere.
https://en.wikipedia.org/wiki/Mars_Climate_Orbiter

📖 Interviewed by doing

THE STORY

Up the ladder, down the ladder. Up the ladder, down the ladder. After a long, hot day cleaning exterior windows in Helena, Montana, and then driving the dusty Rimini Road to the ghost town where my family had moved, I was looking forward to just sitting and watching the sunset.
Jobs were few and college students like me did a wide range of jobs to earn money for next fall's college tuition.

Ten-Mile Creek flowed out of Chessman Reservoir, following the roadway in the narrow canyon; the creek's water level was very, very low. It looked more like a collection of dry river rock than a creek. Trees and grasses were perpetually thirsting for a downpour.

Dry lightning had swept through the night before, but despite an abundance of flash and much noise, the rainfall was only virga -- rain that falls into extremely dry air, evaporating before hitting the earth below.

On the Rimini Road drivers must give full attention to the task because the gravel road is heavily wash-boarded and rich in potholes. A local joke is that if you drive in a straight line and ignore the wash-boarding and potholes, the sheriff will give you a ticket for driving under the influence.

The canyon is deep and loses direct sun mid-afternoon.

Rounding a curve, dodging the potholes and bumps, I saw a wisp of smoke rising far up on a hill to my right. I knew the road well. There were no campgrounds or houses or roads near the thin column of smoke. It looked like morning fog rising as a new day starts and the air heats up. But this was late in the afternoon on a hot, dry day. The wispy, gray column was definitely not fog rising.

So, I pulled the car over to the side and parked. Grabbed a shovel and ax from the trunk (residents driving through the National Forest to reach their homes were required to have a shovel and ax in their cars in case of fire). I started climbing up the hill – not as steep as a ladder but very steep.

I had no idea how big the fire might be but suspected that it started after a tree was hit by dry lightning the night before and probably smoldered all day but was not yet flaming.

This was our "back yard" only a few miles from home, so I had a personal interest in "knocking it down" quickly before it turned into a forest fire.

After the steep climb, I reached the other side of the hill, and met three men wearing U.S. Forest Service hardhats. They had been notified about the smoke by a telephone call and had come up from the other side of the hill, arriving about a half-hour before I did.

Indeed, it was a tree smoldering heavily from a lightning strike. They were in the process of taking the tree down. I helped them take it down and then we dug deep into the roots to make certain nothing else was burning there. Sometimes, roots can smolder for months underground before starting another fire.

Once everything was cold and not smoldering or burning, we were comfortable that it was safe to leave the area. The team leader (a ranger from the Helena District) asked how I'd happened to hike up intending to put out the fire on my own. I told him I drove on the Rimini Road daily to work, had an ax and shovel in the trunk, and thought it was my responsibility to take care of the forest, so the 10-mile drive remained green and growing.

The ranger said he was impressed -- that he had seen enough about my initiative and my attitude – and he asked me to come into his district's office and formally apply if I wanted a summer job with the Forest Service.

> • Wildfires: Smoldering combustion of the forest ground does not have the visual impact of flaming combustion; however, it has important consequences for the forest ecosystem.
>
> Smoldering of biomass can linger for days or weeks after flaming has ceased … The slow propagation leads to prolonged heating and might cause sterilizations of the soil or the killing of roots, seeds, and plant stems at the ground level.
>
> • Subsurface fires: Fires occurring many meters below the surface are a type of smoldering event of colossal magnitude. Subsurface fires in coal mines, peat lands and landfills are rare events, but when active they can smolder for very long periods of time (months or years). https://en.wikipedia.org/wiki/Smouldering

Photo by John Fechter

I did. They hired me. It was one of the best jobs I ever had.

I worked there for several summers, hiking into the forest and fighting small fires, being transported with crews to work on large, project fires, and eventually working as a mountaintop, Forest Service tower lookout.

A regular task as lookout was to be on alert during every thunderstorm, marking the map wherever I saw lightning strike, and then watching those spots for days or weeks to make certain they didn't turn into smoldering trees or actual fires.

WHAT WAS THE PROCESS OF DISCOVERY?

Every day we encounter and work with others. By our action/inaction, our words and attitude, those others perceive our motivation, our initiative, and they see our results. Whether we realize it or not, we're not just being observed while doing our jobs and pursuing our personal goals, we're also being "interviewed" as others see what we are doing and how we are doing it.

If you live your values, others notice. Especially when we go out of our way or are inconvenienced by taking time and effort to do what needs doing, prodded by our own values and motivation.

It was lucky for me that I was able to work with that fire crew and put out the smoldering tree. But I still would have done it myself if they hadn't been there. And if I **had** done it by myself, I would still have a tale to tell about a little adventure. Doing something that needed doing, something that I was capable of doing, and something that had value for all who heard my story.

Doing that persistently, whenever opportunity knocks, makes "luck" happen – in my case, leading to a great job for several summers.

LESSONS LEARNED:

1. If you see something that needs attention, action, or help – **do something** if it within your power to make it happen. Live your values.
2. People who do the right thing and jump in when circumstances call for it – whether it's been assigned to them or not – move to the "short list" of people you want on your team. Notice them, *tell them you noticed,* and put opportunities in their path as things develop.

At a days-long, annual conference for the *Human Factors & Ergonomics Society* I noticed that three people who attended a session where I made a presentation were also in other sessions where I was on a panel. There they were again as I was in the audience asking questions and interacting with other researchers. The conference was fun and intellectually stimulating.

Late in the conference they joined me at a dinner session and informed me that they had been sent by their boss to passively interview me. *What did I present? Did I share the recognition with others on my team? How did I work with other people? How did I collaborate professionally?*

They said they were going to recommend that the boss go ahead with the recruiting process. I'd been "interviewed" while just doing my job and they liked what they saw.

Unfortunately, the job would require a relocation.

I had personal reasons to stay in Maryland for my son's education, so I declined the subsequent, formal, job interview at their company's site. But I stayed in contact with and worked with those people professionally on several projects. It was a delight.

HOW YOU CAN DO IT TOO

Live your values. Know yourself. Know your goals. And whatever station in life you have, do the job you have to the best of your ability. Help others to do things that need doing, if you can. "They" are interviewing you -- without either of you realizing it.

With enthusiasm you can recollect and tell the little and big stories about what you saw, your initiative and pleasure in acting when action was needed and recall how your actions made things better.

If you persistently do this, you'll have a rich repertoire of interesting adventures and results. Stories and results that involved others – others who will share the stories in their own re-telling, informally becoming your references as they tell others who may later contact you for the formal interview.

—Fechter—

Persistence pays

THE STORY

My colleague and I were scheduled to make a presentation to the Commanding General of the Rock Island Arsenal. The Rock Island Arsenal is near the Quad Cities of Iowa and Illinois. Moline, Illinois is the largest city in the area. Our flight from Minneapolis was scheduled to leave in the late afternoon. We would stay in a hotel overnight and then make our presentation at 8:30 the next morning. Anyone familiar with the military knows that 8:30 means 8:30 sharp.

About mid-afternoon of the departure date, a big storm blew up in Minneapolis and we had blizzard conditions. Nevertheless, I fought my way out to the airport. I met my colleague there and we went to the check-in counter. The attendant said "Are you kidding. Airplanes can't fly in this kind of weather. Why don't you go and have dinner and check back in one hour?" So, my colleague and I went to one of the airport restaurants and had dinner.

When we checked back in an hour, we were told that the weather had cleared, and our plane had left half an hour ago. Now we panicked. We had to get to Rock Island Arsenal to make that presentation. Our respective bosses were already in a hotel near the Arsenal. We finally impressed upon the airline agent how urgent it was that we get to Rock Island by morning. He said "Well there aren't any good alternatives. The best I can do is get you to St. Louis tonight and then put you on a 4:00am flight from St. Louis to Quad Cities." Since we had no choice, we took it.

The flight to St. Louis was uneventful enough and we got to our hotel there at about 10:00pm. However, to catch a 4:00am flight, we had to get up at about 2:00am. There was a sleet storm in St. Louis during the night and the roads were very slippery. We caught a cab. The cab driver was half inebriated. We thought this was the end of us as he weaved and slid his way through the slippery streets. But he was very pleased. He told us he was proud to be doing his part to "keep the wheels of industry moving." By some miracle, we arrived at the airport safely and caught our flight to Quad Cities. By this time, our schedule was tight, but we thought we could make it. But there was more trouble ahead. In big cities, it is easy to catch a cab. But in Quad Cities, there were no cabs, at least not at that time of day. And there were no cars to rent. Again, we panicked. Finally, one of the airport agents sympathized with our dilemma. He put through a frantic call to a man who was supposed to drive a cab later in the day. The man wasn't about to be on duty that much before his scheduled time. Finally, he conceded but he wasn't happy. He finally got us to the Arsenal complaining all the way.

We walked in the door at 8:25 and met our respective bosses. My colleague's boss was a nerve wreck. My boss was calm and collected. He said, "I told you they would be here."

We went into the meeting room and set up our material. We were ready by 8:30. The Commanding General walked in at 8:30 sharp. Our presentation went well, and it was just another day at the office.

WHAT WAS THE PROCESS OF DISCOVERY?

As we traveled, my colleague and I wondered how much hardship we had to endure. Was it all worth it? We could probably have called ahead and said the blizzard in Minneapolis made it impossible for us to get to the Quad Cities. The meeting could have been rescheduled for a later date.

But as we discussed our situation, we reached the conclusion that we had made a commitment to be there to make the presentation. Our supervisors counted on it and the General wanted to hear the information we had to present. We were not about to break our commitment if there was any possibility we could keep it. The difficult trip had to be endured. We had to persist in our mission.

Over time, I came to realize the importance of persistence in my job. I developed a concept that I called MAINSTREAMING.

I always imagined that I was rowing a boat in a swift, rocky river. There were many crosscurrents trying to smash me into the rocky shoals. People would tell me that I am taking the wrong approach and that I needed to change direction. Other people would put obstacles in my path by resisting change. I always listened to them to see if their ideas would help meet my objectives, but I never let them steer me off course. I had to keep the boat in the mainstream. That's persistence.

LESSONS LEARNED:

Sometimes it takes persistence to make the right things happen. Life is like that. It is not always easy. Many studies show that persistence is the most critical element of success.

Calvin Coolidge

Source: Commons.wikimedia.org

Calvin Coolidge, the 30th president of the United States once said:

"Nothing in the world can take the place of Persistence.

Talent will not; nothing is more common than unsuccessful men with talent. Genius will not; unrewarded genius is almost a proverb.
Education will not; the world is full of educated derelicts.
Persistence and determination alone are omnipotent."

The slogan "Press On" has solved and always will solve the problems of the human race."

HOW YOU CAN DO IT TOO

Anyone can be persistent. It is not a trait that is inherited or learned from a textbook. It is a habit developed day by day. And persistence applies both to short-term projects (such as our travel), and to our success in life in general. It requires one to have a clear, focused objective and the will power to achieve that objective. It requires one to bounce back from disappointments and look at mistakes as opportunities to improve. Most of all, it requires one to hang in there for the long haul.

—Weimerskirch—

When management tells you to do the wrong thing

THE STORY

I went into my local bank to cash a $44 third party check. The check had been made out to my friend who then endorsed it over to me. Despite the fact that I had been a customer of this bank for more than 45 years, the teller said that his instructions prevented him from cashing a third-party check. He explained that my friend would have to be present in order for him (the teller) to cash the check. My friend would have to verify that the signature was in fact his. I explained that my friend lives in Toronto, Canada and it would be very inconvenient to have him fly to Minneapolis just to cash a $44 check. He suggested that I could cash it the next time I saw my friend. I said that would not be within the 180-day period that I had to cash the check. He said that he didn't have any recommendations for me. All he knew was that he could not cash the check.

I left the bank frustrated and called their customer service number. The woman on the other end explained that the bank was trying to tighten up its security practices. Apparently, crooks are in the habit of forging endorsement signatures and then presenting the check as a third-party check. She thought, however, that the local bank should have made an exception for me and cashed the check. So, I went back to the bank and asked to see a personal banker. She said for $44 she was not going to risk losing a customer. She cashed the check for me.

Sometime later, I went into that same bank to get a notary public signature. I was in the process of joining an organization that required proof that I am a United States citizen. They required a notarized color copy of the picture page of my passport. I made a color copy of my passport and took it to the bank to get it notarized. The banker explained that bank rules require that copies must be made right at the bank and, unfortunately, they did not have a color copier. A casual look would have shown him that I had an exact copy of the passport but that wouldn't have been following the rule. He invited me to come back sometime when he would be able to help me. Again, I left the bank frustrated and having to undergo the inconvenience of finding another notary public.

In sharp contrast to the above story, my wife and I recently visited the International Wolf Center in Ely, Minnesota with some friends.

We met at the Center and both parked our cars there. After our visit, we all got into our car to go off and do some other things. We left our friend's car in the Wolf Center parking lot. We had an enjoyable day visiting and doing things together, totally forgetting that we had to get our friend's car out of that parking lot before they close at 6:00pm. We didn't get back to the Wolf Center until 7:30pm. We arrived there to find their gate closed. The gate consisted of two large beams locked together with a chain and padlock. The gate appeared to be locked tight for the night. It was going to be very inconvenient for our friends not to have their car. They were staying at a campground 40 minutes away.

As we approached the gate though, we found that the padlock had not been locked and there was a note. The note explained that they understood that we probably needed the car, so they didn't lock the padlock. They asked us to please lock the gate once we had gotten the car out.

The next morning, my wife and I felt compelled to go back to the Wolf Center and find the person who had done us this big favor. It turned out to be a young woman. I explained to her how much we appreciated what she had done and what a great inconvenience it would have been had we not been able to get that car. She said that she decided to take a gamble that we were honest people. The car had Florida license plates and that could have made her suspicious. But she used common sense and perhaps bent the rule a little bit. She sure made us delighted customers and she was excited about the good deed she had done.

WHAT WAS THE PROCESS OF DISCOVERY?

All organizations need rules and procedures. Otherwise there would be total chaos. But bureaucracy results when rules are blindly followed without the latitude for some judgment. In my case, the teller might have considered the facts that I have been a customer for more than 45 years, that I live right across the street and that the check was for only $44. I was not likely to be a criminal. The teller and the notary public should have been sensitive to my feelings as their customer. They should have brought the matter before a supervisor so that the supervisor could see the impact the rule was having on their customer.

Many times, rules are put into place by upper management who do not realize the impact of the rule as it is applied in practice. But managers do not want to appear to be unreasonable, or worse yet, lacking in intelligence. There needs to be a process in place that provides for some judgment to be applied. That takes two-way communication. Employees should be trained so that they not only know the rule but also why it is important. Employees need to take responsibility to inform management when a rule does not seem reasonable and is having a negative impact on a customer. Ongoing reality checks are important. Rules need to be changed if they are not meeting their intent.

LESSONS LEARNED:

Organizations should create a culture that encourages employees to use judgment in their everyday work. Employees should be motivated to be well informed about their organization's rules and procedures and to question them when they appear to be unreasonable. Customer focus should be the number one priority.

HOW YOU CAN DO IT TOO

If a rule seems unreasonable either to you or your customer, question it. Bring it to the attention of a higher authority. Take the initiative to be well informed about your organization's rules and procedures and why they are important. And listen intently to your customers. If they are getting frustrated, something is wrong.

—Weimerskirch—

Chapter 06
Gaining Knowledge

Kids in the class!

THE STORY

While making a short, promotional video about the *Master of Science in Technology Management* degree at the University of St. Thomas (UST), I was asked, "Why do you teach?" A simple question. Obviously, I teach, and I've been an adjunct for over 30 years. I enjoy it, but I had never been asked aloud, "Why do I teach?"

I thought about the interviewer's question just for a second and knew the answer right away. My answer: "It keeps me young, alive, interested in the world, watching the "radar screen" of new topics and new issues and new knowledge. And I love teaching because there are kids in the class!"

WHAT WAS THE PROCESS OF DISCOVERY?

I only teach engineering graduate students.

Everyone in my classes has already earned a bachelor's degree before they joined a graduate engineering degree program at UST. Typically, most students are in their mid-twenties or -thirties. However, a good number are in their forties and fifties and some are in their sixties. Kids? That's an informal slang term referring to your children. Isn't that demeaning to call these graduate engineering students -- kids?

No. Calling them kids is one of the highest compliments I could make. These are students – diligent, focused, who are giving up their evenings to study and attend classes They don't arrive back home until nine-thirty p.m. after leaving the campus.

But intellectually they are kids – leaning forward in their chairs, bright-eyed, listening and making notations about learning points, asking questions for something not quite clear, and telling their own stories that augment the class lectures and exercises. They are kids who are not afraid to "look funny" as they learn new things, mispronounce concepts, and keep asking why and how.

Kids do that.

No matter their chronological age, these students are young in mind and spirit and enthusiasm. They know they don't know it all, but they want to! And these kids keep me young.

When I read things, or hear things or see things, I don't just comprehend the new information. I hear and read and see those things with a mind to whether and how that knowledge might be useful for the *kids* to know. So, I'm learning just like a kid, so that I can share it with them.

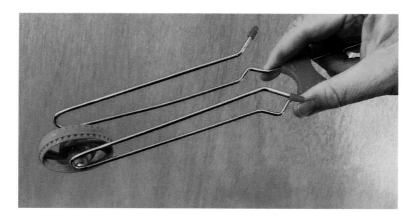

Photo by John Fechter

Engineers look at the world to both understand it and to see issues and problems that might be fixed with some applied science and technologies.

For example, rapid population growth, means that millions may lack adequate access to clean water. Steep population growth curves can create risk for the whole population. Can engineering help to make processes work effectively but use less water? Can engineering solutions find better ways to clean available water and at lower cost, or otherwise reduce the scarcity?

In Japan, Russia, and elsewhere, population growth is slowing below replacement levels unless immigrants make up the difference. Can engineering develop methods, technology, and automation to help caregivers – whose numbers may be inadequate to care for the larger population of elderly? Are there engineering solutions to take over some repetitious tasks and health monitoring so that human caregivers have time to provide personal care that shouldn't or can't be automated?

Seeing the world through my long years of experience helps prioritize significant facts and issues and challenges and opportunities that younger engineers should be aware of, to leverage their knowledge and improve things or mitigate problems.

It is personally interesting for me to learn these new things, but my personal knowledge doesn't change things.

The secret to making change happen is to act -- sharing facts, challenges, tactics, and opportunities with engineers whose careers give them 20, 30, 40 or more years to improve things. That gives me a legacy to know that what I learned, what I tried, what did and didn't work, what I saw, read, or heard will lead to positive changes and mitigate serious problems. I'm still a kid and truly believe that the best is yet to come.

I love teaching because there are kids in the class!"

Applying what you've learned...

I cannot remember the source of this observation, but it is a valuable lesson in enabling people to abandon an outmoded or less effective process and embrace a better process.

Hold a funeral or a memorial ...

Gather the affected members – those who developed or used the old process. Talk about the measurable accomplishments made with the old process – the one being abandoned. Celebrate how that process brought you to today. Thank everyone who developed and used that old process – we wouldn't be where we are today without it.

Then, talk about what has changed and how the old process cannot incorporate all of the changes and new technologies and new expectations.

This "funeral" allows everyone say good things about the way things were and allows them say goodbye to the old ways. Then, it allows them to look forward without regret to the next level of results that will come from the new process.

LESSONS LEARNED:

1. To teach adults is to be an "old scout" on the wagon train, while still being a naïve observer of the world, eager to see what new things might help the wagon train. First, the old scout knows about problems ahead like rivers too deep for the wagons to ford. Second, the scout watches people inventing wagon floats to enable floating instead of fording the river.
2. "Kids" want to learn because they want to do things that they don't yet know how to do. Adult engineers are kids when it comes to the opportunity to learn.

HOW YOU CAN DO IT TOO

If you really want to learn something, to answer the kid within you, then teach it. The enthusiasm of "kids" will give you the psychic energy to go beyond the basics and pursue the refinements that mark a master craftsman rather than an average soul.

You will seek mastery of the topic because your personal pride won't allow you to stand before them teaching unless you have mastered it for yourself.

That means you can be in their shoes as they start to learn it, and a coach to help them develop the refinements beyond the basics.

—Fechter—

Knowledge earns respect

THE STORY

The pocket gophers were having a feast on the plants at my lake cabin. Pocket gophers pile up mounds of dirt while they eat plant roots underground. They leave total devastation.

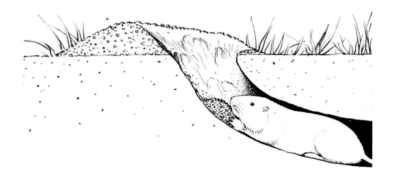

Source: Commons.wikimedia.org

I hire a pest control company and I expected them to take care of the problem. First, I talked to the technician who services my place. He said that he did not have a license to exterminate pocket gophers. Beginning to get frustrated, I called the pest control company main office to see if I could get a licensed technician to take care of the pests. The woman there gave me some vague answers about what my contract covers and what it does not. But she said she would have a supervisor call me.

When the supervisor called me, he explained that state law prohibits them from doing any pest control more than 5 feet from a building. Since my pocket gophers were further out than that, they were prohibited from taking care of my problem. He turned me from a frustrated customer into an understanding -if not a satisfied- customer. I verified that he was telling me the truth.

The point is that the first two people I talked to did not know why they could not take care of my problem. They did not have the knowledge. The third one did, and I respected him for it.

In another case, I was shopping at a nursery for some deer and rabbit resistant perennials. There was a bewildering array of plants to choose from. It was a daunting task to pick out the right plants. I asked several employees for guidance. All they could tell me was that perennials were in this area. Finally, I found an employee who explained to me that plants were arranged in alphabetical order. He pointed out to me that the plants tags tell me whether or not the plant is deer and/or rabbit resistant. That made my job much easier and I was a happy customer

WHAT WAS THE PROCESS OF DISCOVERY?

My wife and I were visiting the Scandinavian countries on a guided tour. When it came to a weekend, we were looking for a church service. We went to the hotel concierge to find out when and where services were held. The concierge said she did not know. When the tour director heard this, she exploded. She said, "I don't know means I don't care and that is not acceptable." She went to the concierge and demanded that the concierge find out the information. Within minutes, we had the information we wanted. Our tour director then went to the hotel manager and told him to give the concierge better training.

LESSONS LEARNED:

Every employee, in the course to their everyday job, comes in contact with people -- usually customers -- who are looking for information and guidance. An answer of "I don't know." means "I don't care." Employees should always be trying to expand their knowledge of their job and environment so that they can respond. This is largely a matter of attitude. The result is that they will receive positive feedback and their job will be more rewarding.

HOW YOU CAN DO IT TOO

Whatever your job, try to be as knowledgeable about it as you can. Pay attention to the questions you are asked on a day-to-day basis. If you don't know the answer, find out. Have a positive attitude. Be aware that an "I don't know" response is a customer dissatisfier.

—Weimerskirch—

Chapter 07
Understanding Human Nature

I can't read cursive

THE STORY

A night owl, my aunt Phoebe used to stay up until 2:00 or 3:00am, and correspondingly didn't start the next day until very late in the morning or even noon.

On this day, she looked out of her window and saw that his truck was still there, next to his trailer. He was a newcomer relocating to Orcas Island in northwest Washington state, near the Canadian border.

Earlier in the week she had given him permission to park his trailer on her lot, while he searched for a job in Eastsound, Washington, on Orcas Island. And, happening in the days before everyone had a cell phone, she agreed that he could give potential employers her landline telephone number to get ahold of him.

Good news had happened. Yesterday afternoon a man had called to leave a message. "Tell him he has the job and needs to be here tomorrow at 8:00 a.m., sharp."

Despite her advanced age, she had beautiful penmanship. She carefully wrote him a note, describing the time, date, who had called, and the message, "… you have the job and need to be there tomorrow at 8:00 a.m. sharp." She walked carefully and slowly over to his trailer and taped the note to the trailer's door.

But now, as Phoebe woke up it was very late in the morning of "tomorrow", but his truck was still there.

He was in the trailer, not at work.

She left her house, again walking carefully and slowly to the trailer, and knocked on the door until he opened it up.

"Why are you still home? You're supposed to be at work. He called yesterday and said you were supposed to be there at 8:00 a.m."

"How would I know that?"

"I left a note on your trailer door yesterday, with all of the details."

"Oh. I saw the note, but I can't read cursive handwriting."

Hearing my aunt tell this story, we both did a "Tsk, tsk," worrying about the limitations he would experience when searching for a job, then finding work, and eventually doing his job at work.

WHAT WAS THE PROCESS OF DISCOVERY?

Years passed. And the story faded away.

But it came back to life when two pairs of engineering, graduate students come up to me after an evening class session had just ended. I had hand-written multiple suggestions, notes, and comments on the first draft of all team reports and handed the noted papers back to students during the class. Now I had two teams waiting with their critiqued drafts. They wanted to discuss the feedback.

"OK, what kinds of things do you want to ask or talk about?" I asked.

One of them replied, "We need you to go through all of your handwritten comments. None of us can read cursive writing."

I was startled. How could these graduate engineers have completed their bachelor's degrees in the 21st century without learning how to use and read cursive handwriting? The answer was obvious – their thumbs were fluent in texting and Siri or Alexa listened for their verbal commands.

Their notes made during class were all captured via keyboard entries on their laptops. And their library research was done online, accessing databases throughout the world, and then their bibliography was summarily formatted automatically using RefWorks®.

<u>LESSONS LEARNED:</u>

I cannot assume that the common things I've learned and the experiences I've had are universally known and understood or even still applicable in today's world.

We are separated from one another by geography, by the eras I have lived in versus the eras lived in by other people, by the contrast of village life, metropolitan life, or country life. And so on.

Cultural awareness. It's more than just knowing that people call carbonated beverages "pop" in some parts of the USA, while in other parts of the country people say "soda."

It's more.

As noted in an online blog, **whatsthepont** "...some good advice from Fons Trompenaars at Academi Wales Summer School, "If you want to understand your own culture, you need to spend some time in someone else's culture"

HOW YOU CAN DO IT TOO

In the case of cursive handwriting, it's more than knowing that *cursive handwriting competency* is no longer "a given fact".

By Rob C. Croes / Anefo - Nationaal Archief 933-4299 (cropped), CC BY-SA 3.0 nl, https://commons.wikimedia.org/w/index.php?curid=2810173

Vigdís Finnbogadóttir served as the fourth President of Iceland -- **for 16 years**, a role model for women and girls.

She noted the story of a young Icelandic boy in her country seeing Ronald Reagan on TV and asking in confusion, "Mommy, can a man be president?"

Some nostalgic regrets as I learned that. But also, some serious impediments to career advancement if one is unable to read notes and correspondence from the past. The "we can't read cursive" comment startled me, just as receiving my comments written in cursive startled them.

Neither is right or wrong.
But we all must keep visiting places and circumstances and having experiences that are not "just like us."

If you want to understand your own culture, you need to leave your own and spend some time in someone else's culture. As technology shifts, as demographics change, as companies are bought and sold, and as the nature of commerce and socializing constantly change, proactively visit those other places – take notes – and write down (in cursive, if you can) what's been lost and what's been added when those cultural changes enter your world.

—Fechter—

Who pays the price?

THE STORY

It was to be an exciting trip, my first international venture beyond Canada or Mexico.

For the first time, the *International Ergonomics Association* was holding its congress behind the "Iron Curtain". It was a big, big deal.

To many, it was another sign that scientists and managers in countries behind the "Iron Curtain" were rejoining international, professional societies as peers.

The Polish Post Office issued a special postage stamp (see sidebar), and the organizers within Poland were given many resources never before made available for such a meeting – including paid support staff and regular use of a Mercedes Benz for transportation.

I had no competency in the Polish language and bought an LP (long-

Ergonomists study human capabilities in relation to the demands of work.

Wojciech Bogumil Jastrzębowski, (1799-1882) was a Polish scientist, naturalist, inventor, professor of botany, physics, zoology and horticulture in Warsaw. One of the fathers of ergonomics, he created the word in a philosophical narrative, (The Outline of Ergonomics, i.e. Science of Work, Based on the Truths Taken from the Natural Science). He derived the term from two Greek words: "ergon", meaning work and "nomoi", meaning natural laws.

https://en.wikipedia.org/wiki/Wojciech_Jastrz%C4%99bowski

playing) vinyl record [this was in 1979] to acquaint me with Polish and its pronunciation.

I was working at the National Bureau of Standards (now NIST – National Institute of Standards and Technology) and would be traveling on a "Brown" passport as a U.S. government employee.

In preparation for the trip, I was briefed by the CIA.

Traveling on a "Brown" passport I should expect to be followed everywhere, and I would likely be photographed many times -- while at the congress, while walking around Warsaw and other towns, while in the hotel and restaurants.

I was instructed -- DO NOT go into anyone's hotel room, especially females, because you will be photographed, and everything said will be recorded.

In 1976, travelers shared many anecdotes about being observed and recorded while visiting countries in the Soviet Bloc. One US official and his wife were traveling in Poland and kept up a positive , public front despite some experiences.

But upon returning to their hotel room, the wife remarked aloud in frustration, "This is so frustrating sometimes! I just wish they at least had a waste basket in our room!!"

In minutes, there was a knock on the door and the maid brought in a wastebasket. The couple was subdued, realizing their room was bugged with a microphone.

Be an active participant in the IEA Congress, but be constantly aware before you say things to anyone that you are a government employee and it would be to their advantage if they recorded something compromising that could be used against you or the US at a future date.

Ok. Ok. But I was still excited to go.

As the plane touched down in Warsaw, it was met by a military truck filled with **very** young soldiers. They jumped out of the truck and lined the pathway from the airplane to the airport arrivals hall. Each soldier stood at attention. Each was armed with a rifle which they held at the ready with both hands.

I remember how stark the airport was, with only a few bare bulbs outside, and a few, old taxis waiting. After passing through customs and immigration, and after declaring the amount of US currency in my wallet, I was brushed ahead and out. I took a taxi and told him my hotel destination. He asked "dollars?" "Yes" "Five dollars, then."

It was a bargain because I was paying just $5 in American currency.

There were no television displays at the airport, no internet, no smartphones, only paper newspapers and magazines. I checked in at the hotel, and then looked in the lobby store to see if there were any magazines or newspapers available to bring me up to date.

Yes, but the only publication in English was a *Worker's Party* newspaper from the U.K.

Television was available only in a central lounge at the hotel and only on for selected hours. Knowing no Polish, I watched what I could visually interpret. It was a grainy film about military training and maneuvers in case NATO invaded Poland and the Poles and the Russians had to repel the attack.

Poland was a country in recovery and transition. Horse-drawn farmer's wagons used automobile tires to replace the old, iron and wooden wheels.

Many buildings in Warsaw still showed long series of chips in the bricks and stone where aircraft machine guns had strafed up and down and left and right. And little, wall-mounted memorials with fresh flowers and small Polish flags were mounted on building walls on many city blocks.

The IEA congress had arranged a bus tour to Łódź, Poland to visit medical facilities, some manufacturing sites, and fabric mills. We were all ergonomics professionals; our "back home" occupations were aimed at improving worker safety and efficiency.

During the bus ride, we asked about occupational safety, accidents, and injuries – and what was being done to protect Polish workers on the job in medical settings, manufacturing settings, and the fabric mills – lots of questions about worker safety in general. It was a normal topic when ergonomics people get together, trying to pick up tips about keeping workers as safe as possible while doing their jobs.

We had seen and commented aloud about many anecdotal examples of risky behaviors we'd seen during our Łódź-area visits. For example, chemical exposure, dangerous and precarious positioning of people using heavy machinery, and limited sight views as equipment and materials moved within buildings. That brought up comments about mining safety, traffic accidents, agricultural accidents.

After a few hours of this chit-chat on the bus as we moved through the Polish countryside, our "handler tour guide" took a long drag on his cigarette after we had asked a few direct questions about safety. He stood up, steadying himself as the bus bounced a bit on the road.

We passengers waited for his answer about workplace safety, injuries, accidents, and deaths.

Speaking carefully and assertively, he told us that
Polish workers – especially in mining -- were
devoting their lives to bringing Poland back to being
a great culture and a strong economy – and that
their work had the intensity of war. Deaths and
injuries were to be considered "casualties of war."
Once victorious, after the economy had recovered and
was once again powerful, *then* Poland could invest
time to improve worker safety. Until then, it was war
– worker safety sometimes had to be sacrificed for
the good of the nation. It was the price Poland had to
pay to regain its position.

He stopped. Sat down, took another long drag on his
cigarette, and looked out the front window at the
country scenery.

His comments were stunning. The bus was silent. No
more questions aloud. We quietly said a few things to
one another, but the open forum was over.

We silently watched the countryside out the window.
Taxi drivers sitting on the curb, plucking sunflower
seeds from giant sunflower heads for a snack. More
of those flat wagons on regular rubber tires with
automobile wheels, hauling farm supplies down the
road, powered by a single horse.

Who pays the price? Did the workers know they were
in an economic "war", and that they were considered
expendable? Was the economic situation truly so dire
that expenses for better training and safety were
unaffordable?

At the national level, were workers soldiers? At the
company level, were workers expendable to achieve
company financial goals – goals that those workers
themselves would be unlikely to benefit from
personally?

An Iron Curtain has descended...

Winston Churchill's **"Sinews of Peace"** address of 5 March 1946, at Westminster College in Fulton, Missouri, used the term "iron curtain" in the context of Soviet-dominated Eastern Europe.

"From Stettin in the Baltic to Trieste in the Adriatic, an iron curtain has descended across the Continent. Behind that line lie all the capitals of the ancient states of Central and Eastern Europe. Warsaw, Berlin, Prague, Vienna, Budapest, Belgrade, Bucharest and Sofia; all these famous cities and the populations around them lie in what I must call the Soviet sphere, and all are subject, in one form or another, not only to Soviet influence but to a very high and in some cases increasing measure of control from Moscow."

https://en.wikipedia.org/wiki/Iron_Curtain

WHAT WAS THE PROCESS OF DISCOVERY?

When we departed for the tour, we had all unknowingly assumed that the rules and expectations and values we brought with us were rules and expectations and values mostly shared by everyone, everyplace.

I still consider the "handler tour guide's" perspective to be wrong – that reaching Poland's national economic position and goals were the only goals that mattered, no matter the near-term cost to lives and health. But once said aloud, we pondered things.

Years later I had the words to say – that Poland's national economic position and goals would be better and faster met if worker safety was a non-negotiable criterion instead of considering worker issues to be collateral damage. That is, preventing the things that caused worker death and injury would require process improvement. And those process improvements would simultaneously accelerate achieving the national economic position and goals.

If we simply accept that the way we do things today is the only way, then whatever defects, costs, damages, or injuries that happen will persistently accompany today's process.

But we can change the process. Doing things differently -- to deliver the same, good things as delivered using the old method, but doing the process in a new way without unnecessary costs and dangers. If both worker safety and productivity are non-negotiable, must-haves, then change the process you use to ensure **both** are delivered.

Yes, **we can** achieve both goals at the same time. This seems counterintuitive to most people, but it is true.

This was demonstrated to work extremely well when Paul O'Neill (US Treasury Secretary, chairman and CEO of Alcoa, chairman of the RAND Corporation) became CEO of Alcoa and had safety as the first item on the agenda for **every** meeting.

He set goals of zero lost workdays. People thought he was naïve. In the end, he may not have achieved zero, but he achieved far more than he would have if he'd settled for a less aggressive goal. Alcoa dropped from 1.86 lost workdays to injury per 100 workers to 0.20. That rate fell to 0.125 by 2012. Profits increased five-fold over his tenure.

LESSONS LEARNED:

Sometimes, things need to be said aloud because what we *assume* to be true may not be true to everyone. Or worse – unstated to ourselves – our assumptions about shared truths may be ignored by others who see a larger game at play.

Mission, vision, values, and goals said aloud become reference points. Saying them aloud and looking at today's situation through the filter of what we said aloud can expose gaps that must be closed in order to turn those mission, vision, values, goal statements into facts rather than just aspirations.

In a transparent organization, motives are clear because there are no hidden missions, no hidden visions, no hidden values, and no hidden goals.

HOW YOU CAN DO IT TOO

No one expects to go to work and never return. No one expects to return home from work injured. Say that aloud.

If you see something that conflicts with that, where today's way of doing things accepts death or injury or damage or defects as occasional accompaniments to a process, say aloud that it's wrong, and then find a solution.

Within your organization, go on a Gemba walk. Go to where the work is being done. Watch.
Watch.
Watch.

Only then, ask why and how things are being done. Ask what measures inform everyone – what are the measures they use to know that things are happening as planned and as expected.

Gemba walk -- personal observation of work – where the work is happening.

Don't assume. Ask why.

Don't assume. Ask why.

—Fechter—

Understanding global cultures

THE STORY

I never learned a second language. It would have been helpful, but I never had or took the time to do it. It is difficult to learn a second language if you do not do it when you are young. But, while being able to speak a second language would have been helpful, I discovered that understanding different global cultures is even more important. A few stories will illustrate the point.

I made a trip to Japan, during which we visited several companies. As we concluded each visit, one of the travelling team would deliver the "greeting." The greeting is a thank you to the hosting company for the time and effort they spent on our visit. One morning, our tour guide asked me if I would deliver the greeting that afternoon after our visit. One of our travelling group had a Berlitz book of the Japanese language. I borrowed it with the intent of learning one sentence that I could deliver during my greeting that afternoon. I soon learned just how difficult the Japanese language really is. About noon, our translator can up to me and said "Arnie, I heard what you are planning to do. Don't do it. The Japanese language has so many subtleties and innuendoes that you may be saying something entirely different from what you intend. You may insult them. You tell me the words in English, and I will translate them into Japanese." The words I opened with were "Today we have visited a truly world-class company." As our translator spoke those words in Japanese, I could see the President light up like a Christmas tree. He was obviously pleased. That evening, our translator told me "You could not have chosen better words when you called them world-class. Because, while you may look at them that way, in the Japanese culture, they are too modest to regard themselves as world-class." So, I didn't learn the Japanese language, but I did learn a lesson in culture.

Then there was my trip to China. My wife had asked me, if I got a chance during my leisure time, to buy some "Beanie Babies" which were a popular stuffed toy at the time. They were made in Beijing and were much cheaper in China than in the United States. So, one night we had a chance to visit Silk Alley. Silk Alley is a tightly packed outdoor bazaar with hundreds of vendors. A lady on the trip was also looking for Beanie Babies. We encountered a group of American college students, so we asked them how to say Beanie Baby in Chinese. They said there probably is no literal translation of Beanie Baby but maybe "baby toy" would do. So, we said OK how do we say baby toy in Chinese. They gave us a word that sounded phonically like SHA-HEIZA-WAAN-JU. So, we went up and down Silk Alley saying SHA-HEIZA-WAAN-JU? SHA-HEIZA-WAAN-JU? As we passed one booth, I heard a man say, "That man speaks perfect Chinese." And we did find some Beanie Babies. So, without knowing a word of Chinese, we did accomplish our objective. Language barriers can be overcome.

In my job, I had assembled a group of Honeywellers from around the world. Collectively, we had the job of managing Honeywell's quality program. At the beginning, many of the group felt that international cultural differences would prevent us from implementing a uniform program in Honeywell units around the globe. So, one day, I took some time out of our three-day meeting to ask the non-U.S. participants what irritated them about us -- Americans.

Some of the things they brought up were:

- when we call at 3:00pm Minneapolis time, not stopping to think that that is nighttime elsewhere in the world
- they resented being called "foreign operations." In the U.S., we frequently refer to "domestic" and "foreign" operations. They said, "We don't look upon ourselves as foreigners."
- when we forget that not all countries operate on the same electrical voltage and frequency that the U.S. does.
- and the list goes on.

What their comments had in common was an attitude of unconscious arrogance on the part U.S. Honeywellers. They felt that U.S. Honeywellers didn't really look upon international Honeywellers as equals.

WHAT WAS THE PROCESS OF DISCOVERY?

Over time, I discovered that the things people have in common are much stronger than things that make us different. The desire to do challenging work, to help improve our company, and to make a good life for our families was much more powerful than the artificial differences we may have had. The color of our skin, the language we speak, or our cultural backgrounds are much less important than the fundamental dignity of all human beings. Once we came to this understanding, we were able to implement a uniform quality program around the world.

Source: Commons.wikimedia.org

LESSONS LEARNED:

There is more to global communications than just language. Culture is important. The customs and values of people differ from country to country. Understanding those customs and values is a perquisite to effective communications and relationships.

Sometimes cultures and value systems come into conflict with each other. On a trip to India, I was at lunch one day. I was somewhat offended when my local host snapped his fingers and motioned for "the boy" to open my bottle of water for me. Later in the lunch, my napkin dropped off my lap onto the floor. I reached down to pick it up. Again, the local host said, "The boy will pick it up." I said 'That's OK. I can pick it up myself." I may have offended him, but I was, in turn, offended by the idea of a servant having to do menial tasks that I could do myself. My value system overruled culture in this case.

HOW YOU CAN DO IT TOO

Take time to dig deeper than the language barrier. Get to know the customs and values of people from other countries. Get to know how they think and why they act the way they do. And above all, treat everyone as a worthwhile human being.

—Weimerskirch—

I thought you spoke English

THE STORY

"Your English accent is very difficult to understand."

It was our first French barbeque, and unfortunately, our last because shortly after this trip I changed companies and no longer had occasion to travel regularly to France for business.

During the workday my wife visited *The Louvre Museum*, the royal chapel of *Sainte-Chapelle*, the *Sacré-Cœur Basilica* and other famous sites while I worked with product developers and production line supervisors at their facilities.

At the end of the week we received a special treat. A Parisian colleague hosted us for a French BBQ at his home.

His 30-something daughter joined the BBQ and sat quietly, listening, for most of the late afternoon and evening. Then, after we were long finished with the meal and just talking, his daughter spoke up. She was polite and cordial but said that she had to admit that she was very disappointed. She had hoped to brush up on her English and learn some American idioms during our visit.

But, with a serious and slightly sad tone, she said she had had a very difficult time understanding us because our English was so unusual and strongly accented.

My wife and I are both native-born Americans who speak English as our first language. Maybe with a Montana pace and accent. We do say "crik" instead of "creek" and "pop" instead of "soda", but otherwise our English is standard American – the kind taught to and used by radio broadcasters across the nation.

Her French father was eyebrow-raising surprised. He asked for examples. She gave several. He started to laugh a bit. He asked for other examples and she gave several more. His laugh became strong and hearty with some little tears on the edge of his eyes. He had served in the French Army in Algeria and his demeanor was normally much more reserved, almost stoic.

This laughter was a treat for us all. They had normally conversed in the family in French, so he'd had little opportunity to hear her speak English. She was becoming upset, thinking he was laughing *at* her.

He was not.

He stopped laughing and asked her to say a few phrases in English. She was laughing in sympathy – not because she understood exactly why, but because his sincere laughter was infectious to us all.

It was not until he heard her speak so much in English –this evening – that he realized that she had honed her spoken English while living in Kenya. In Kenya, written English can be identical to a document written in London or Minneapolis. But the spoken version of that written text – in Kenya – often comes with such a strong accent as to be nearly unrecognized by people outside of Kenya. Similar confusion hearing New Zealand English, or a strong Scottish or Irish brogue...

She had lectured us that our English was very, very difficult to understand because we spoke with such an unusual accent. And she clearly communicated that she felt the time together had been for naught because our spoken English was terrible.

Her father explained that his laughter was provoked by her stern critique and disappointment that our spoken English was so poor, when in fact our spoken form was typical of what she would hear throughout England, Canada, and America. Hundreds of millions of people.

She had a wonderful, sweetheart personality and accepted her father's gentle comments with a blushing smile. With this conversation she realized that the Kenyan English accent was not the worldwide norm; she had learned it perfectly during her cultural immersion while living in Kenya.

We entertained one another for a bit of fun as she would say a phrase in Kenyan English and ask us to repeat it in American English. And we'd do the same, saying a phrase in American English and asking her to say it in Kenyan English.

> An old joke:
> What do you call someone who speaks three languages?   *Trilingual.*
> What about a person who speaks two languages? *Bilingual.*
> And what's the term for someone who speaks only one language? *American.* 😊

WHAT WAS THE PROCESS OF DISCOVERY?

It's often said that one does not know their own culture until they leave it.

Some differences are obvious, such as a country's standard to drive on the right or the left of the roadway. Some are more subtle, like the caution to not bring your German sweetheart yellow and white chrysanthemums because they are given only for funerals.

The 30-something daughter at the BBQ had learned and spoken French from birth. She learned English by spending years living in Kenya.

She left the French and Kenyan cultures at our BBQ, hearing her parents speak English as a second language and hearing us speak English as we would in America.

She didn't know American culture from personal experience, so she had assumed that her Kenyan English perspective could be generalized to America. Hence, her conclusion that we were not typical Americans because our American English was so much different from her Kenyan English experience.

LESSONS LEARNED:

In an earlier time, the lesson learned would be that people can have a distorted – inaccurate – picture of the real world because they see it through an ethnocentric lens.

She thought that the accent in Kenyan English was the worldwide norm

William G. Sumner, Yale, held America's first professorship in sociology. He defined **ethnocentrism** as "the technical name for the view of things in which one's own group is the center of everything, and all others are scaled and rated with reference to it."

when in reality it differed dramatically from Canadian or American English – which differs dramatically from New Zealand English.

With today's social media and algorithm-generated news feeds, we must be aware of and work consciously try to avoid living in a Filter Bubble -- where what we read or hear or see is fed to us by filtering algorithms to match what we already think and feel, rather than being a true and full picture of life and the real world.

> *Filter bubble* – a term coined by Internet activist Eli Pariser – is a state of intellectual isolation that allegedly can result from personalized searches when a website algorithm selectively guesses what information a user would like to see based on information about the user, such as location, past click-behavior and search history. Wikipedia,
> https://en.wikipedia.org/wiki/Filter_bubble

HOW YOU CAN DO IT TOO

My recommendation for you is easy to say, but takes hard, steady work to make it happen.

That is, develop a questions filter.

Give it a fancy name to make you think it through when you use it. Your question, *Is my view accurate?* Put it in German to make it sound official, *Ist meaner Ansicht richtig?* or French to make it sound nuanced, *Mon opinion est-elle exacte?*

And during the course of the day, notice when you make a decision – is it happening by habit, has the world changed since you last encountered similar decision points, would you reach the same decision if dealing with people in Iceland or Mozambique?

The point is not to slow you down. Rather, to help you ensure that the world you knew is the world of now.

—Fechter—

Chapter 08
Thinking Outside the Box

📖 Testing the limits
— a Parisian dinner

THE STORY

I originally wrote a version of this story for a celebratory sendoff when a colleague was retiring. We gave him a collection of stories from years of working together. He was a smart, very reserved friend. But his tolerance and diplomacy were sorely tested when three of us had dinner together at **The Tides Wharf Restaurant** in Bodega Bay, California.

We'd had a very good day presenting Lean Sigma training at a plant site in Santa Rosa, California. As an end of training treat, we three drove west to the Pacific Ocean, to Bodega Bay, site of Alfred Hitchcock's famous film, "The Birds". The meal was excellent, and as we waited for dessert, something was mentioned that reminded me of an interesting experience I'd had in Paris.

The other two were listening closely, leaning into the conversation and following my words.

Here's the story, and their reactions...

I was in Paris for a worldwide, senior executive meeting of our company at its Paris headquarters. We were into our 3rd day of meetings at the Hotel Concorde Lafayette and at the end of a long day we were all going to a fancy Parisian restaurant for a group dinner—executives and several spouses.

None of us had cars so we went to the restaurant by taxis -- multiple taxis. Some, but not all of the visitors spoke French. So, we needed to make sure there was a French speaker present in each taxi to talk with the driver.

I was shepherding the mixing and matching of taxi riders and after everyone else had been driven away, I found myself at the end with an English couple (he spoke French, but his wife did not), a very small taxi, and myself. The couple fit snugly into the back seat, but there was no room for me in the back. I looked in the front seat and the taxi driver saw that I was dismayed – the back seat was full and both front seats were occupied.

He smiled broadly and said in English "ma fille, my girl. She can sit on your lap. Is OK?"

Heck, I was in Paris; business was over for the day, so I agreed. I got in, she sat on my lap, the door closed, and we were off.

As I was telling this story in California to my colleagues, they were both a little surprised. "She sat on your lap?!"
"Yes. **And was she CUTE!** Closest I'd been to such a cutie, much less have her sit on my lap"

Listening to this story in Bodega Bay, California, my colleagues looked at each other and started acting a little uncomfortable.

But I continued…

"Yes, the English woman sitting in the back seat with her husband was a little huffy, but I was happy with my circumstances and ignored the attitude being glared at me from the back seat."

And we were off. She looked up at me, didn't make a sound, but rested her head on my shoulder. She kissed my ear. The driver smiled and laughed. She looked at him, then looked back at me (I am not very fluent in French) and she kissed me again and rested her head.

The English lady in the back harrumphed. Her spouse just laughed.

As I described this, my California colleagues looked at each other and were now becoming very uncomfortable. They politely commented about the scenery outside, trying to change the subject. But I resumed the story.

One colleague was perplexed that I continued and that I ignored their hints and discomfort. "John!" and then she looked over at my other colleague, smiling politely but not really, saying to him "Can you believe he's telling this to us?!!!"

My reserved male colleague suggested that maybe I might go on to another topic. But I smiled, and said, "This isn't the good part yet. Let me tell you more."

They were now deeply uncomfortable. We were many miles from Santa Rosa, I had the car and the keys, our dessert was not yet at the table, and I insisted on telling the tale. The story sounded very much out of character from me, and that was obviously confusing to them.

Back to Paris…

The taxi drove up to the traffic circle that surrounds the famous and beautiful Arc de Triomphe. Traffic was heavy and slow. Much starting and stopping. And then the taxi in front of us made a sudden, full stop and our taxi hit its taillight.

The driver's girl started sliding off my lap, but I had my arms around her and kept her from hitting anything in the sudden stop. The driver looked at me, and I said, "C'est bon. It's OK".

He jumped out to go yell colorful language with the other driver.

She was wiggling and moving and trying to get out to join him, but I kept my arms around her. So, she relaxed and watched the colorful, arm-waving argument with the rest of us.

But she was very anxious, looking at him, looking at me, giving me a kiss and looking back at him. The English woman in the back seat was upset at the small accident, complaining about the delay, and about how she couldn't believe I had his girl sitting on my lap while she nuzzled and kissed me, and the driver just accepted it.

Listening to the story, my California colleagues now were becoming really upset. He strongly suggested that maybe I should go to something else. She speechless and then harrumphing like the English spouse as I persisted in telling my tale.

They both commented that their impressions of me had totally changed and that we should probably go home right now. They were unhappy and confused. This was all so out of character for me to be relating such a story.

So, I continued.

I related how the driver got back into the taxi, smiled at her, reached over to give her a little squeeze while saying "mon chéri", then smiling at me saying "merci", gave her a hug with his hand, and were off to the restaurant.

In a few minutes we were there. The English couple got out. I paid the fare, and the taxi driver's girl, his

sweetheart, gave me a last kiss, and the petite chien
– his girl – his little poodle dog – jumped from my
arms to his and kissed him all over his face.

At this point in Bodega Bay, my California
colleagues broke out into laughter and smiles and
extraordinary relief that they had misinterpreted the
story – helped much by the way I told the tale. They
thought "his girl" was a woman, not a cute, little
poodle.

My reserved, male colleague's relief was palpable. He
gave a long exhale. She kept saying, "I couldn't
believe you kept telling us more and more. It was all
so strange. You were so relaxed and kept talking and
we kept looking at each other trying to get you to
stop because we thought ... well I thought --
everything I knew about you was wrong. That is such
a funny story".

We had a delightful ride back to Santa Rosa. I
related how many times "previously upset people"
had forced me to tell the story to others while those
"previously upset" people watched the new listeners
go through the same incredulous discomfort and then
break out in laughter that "his girl" was a poodle.

WHAT WAS THE PROCESS OF DISCOVERY?

Upon arrival at the restaurant in Paris, some people
at my table asked why we arrived late and if there
had been an argument -- because the English
colleague's wife seemed slightly upset. I described
what had happened, with the accident, and in my
telling I used the phrase "his girl."

<u>"Juxtaposition of the incongruous."</u>

Many, many years ago, in high school, Father E.J. was lecturing to our class about several religious principles -- when one student laughed out loud. E.J. had not intended to make a joke, so he departed from his lecture and asked, "What was so funny that it made you laugh out loud?"

The student explained that he'd taken the wrong meaning for a term E. J. had just used, and that the unintended double-meaning made the statement unintentionally funny.

E.J. then took advantage of this "teachable moment" to explain theories of humor. A general rule about humor was that people saw something as funny when there was a "juxtaposition of the incongruous." That is, two things that don't go together – it's the punch line of a joke that catches us by surprise because everything up to that juxtaposition of the incongruous was leading us in one direction and we are suddenly pulled to an incongruous situation. For example, ""Is the doctor at home?" the patient asked in his bronchial whisper. "No," the doctor's young and pretty wife whispered in reply. "Come right in." from Victor Raskin in "Semantic Mechanisms of Humor", 1985, p.100.

I do not remember anything else from his lecture that day, but I have never forgotten "juxtaposition of the incongruous."

Someone heard me say "his girl" and thought that I had my arms around the taxi driver's girlfriend. And the story took off from there. In my multiple tellings and refinements over the next week or so in Paris, I honed the delivery and the pacing to intentionally lead listeners one way, knowing that laughter that would follow when I concluded with the punch line about his girl being a little dog, not a taxi driver's human girlfriend.

Upon arrival back in Minneapolis I was met by my wife, and we drove home together, talking happily about my trip. When I started telling her the story, the mood changed and she became so angry that her face turned red and she looked out the passenger window, refusing to make eye contact with me.

Then, when I finished the story and she understood it was a petite chien – little dog -- and not a woman, my wife laughed so hard she had tears in her eyes.

Upon telling the story back at the office, people had the same experience – anger and hostility that my behavior "with his girl in the taxi" was out of character and out of place – and then that anger dissolved into smiles and laughter. Beyond that, I was pulled by several people into other senior executive offices and meetings to tell "the story."

I obliged and realized how useful the story was to keep everyone's attention while I talked also about the successful partnership and negotiating sessions we had had. It would have taken weeks for those trip decision and action item highlights to be read and acted upon if I had used only a traditional trip report.

LESSONS LEARNED:

The story was funny. And – if they endured until the end of the story -- its humor served as a useful icebreaker when starting new projects with people speaking other languages and living in other cultures.

HOW YOU CAN DO IT TOO

In your day, listen for the juxtaposition of the incongruous. You'll find many examples. Note them and save them, though probably not as lengthy as my Paris story! Many of them can be useful examples to safely point out and clarify everyday misunderstandings -- in a safe way that doesn't make the persons involved lose face.

—Fechter—

The obvious isn't always obvious

THE STORY

The crickets were coming in from the courtyard into the hallway of our apartment building. They were creeping under the door. When they got in, the pesticide would kill them. But not before they had migrated 20 or 30 feet into the building. So, the hallway was littered with dead crickets and they were left there for days at a time. It was a rather revolting mess.

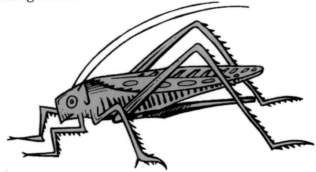

Source: publicdomainpictures.net

Residents complained about the situation, wondering why nobody cleaned them up. The cleaning lady offered to do that but was told by management that it was not her job. Occasionally, someone would clean them up, but they would come right back. Someone had the idea that cleaning carts and maintenance carts could carry hand-held vacuum cleaners and the crickets could just be vacuumed up as the cart went by. It would take almost no time and the hallway would be kept clean. One woman put tape at the bottom of her apartment door to prevent the crickets from getting in. One kind lady even put the crickets back outside. None of the solutions were implemented by management and so the problem continued.

Finally, someone had the idea to install a new sweep (shield) on the bottom of the outside door to prevent the crickets from getting in in the first place. That worked and the problem was prevented.

WHAT WAS THE PROCESS OF DISCOVERY?

Why did it take so long to solve this problem? Apparently because the human mind is intuitively programmed to solve problems, not to prevent them. Everyone was thinking about how to clean up the crickets, not how to prevent them from getting in in the first place.

There is a mental process going on here that is worth thinking about. In technical terms, it is called "robust design." In essence, it means that products and processes should be designed so that they work right under any condition and in the simplest way. In the case of the crickets, the door should have been designed to keep critters out even in the cold weather when they attempt to get into a warmer building.

LESSONS LEARNED:

The human mind intuitively tries to solve problems after they occur. The concept of robust design prevents problems before they occur. Brainstorming is the key to robust design.

Brainstorming can be done individually or in focus groups. A great example of brainstorming is the invention of McDonald's Egg McMuffin.

Another example will illustrate the principle of robust design. In my first house, I had a humidifier to moisten the air in the house on cold winter days. It was a complex device with two motors. One turned a wet sponge rubber drum in a water reservoir. The other motor powered a fan that sucked air through the wet sponge rubber drum, moistened it, and blew it back into furnace plenum chamber. It was a complicated system that required lots of maintenance.

One day, a friend of mine said "You know, there is a much better way of doing this." Based on his recommendation, I installed a system that had no moving parts. It relied on the fact that, on a forced air furnace, there is a pressure differential between the hot air plenum and the cold air return. Air can be pulled by that pressure differential through a moist media to humidify it and then be blown back into the house. No moving parts and very little maintenance.

Why didn't the original humidifier designers think of that? They were locked into conventional thinking and were not open to the possibilities.

Source: Wikipedia.org

The operator of a McDonald's franchise in Santa Barbara, California wanted a fast-food breakfast he could serve before 11:00am. He and his assistant tried many crazy ideas. One of them was to cook an egg with a broken yoke in a round plastic ring. Then they put it inside a muffin. They presented their idea to then McDonald President Ray Kroc. At first, Ray

Kroc thought it was a crazy idea, making a hamburger out of an egg. But it caught on and the rest is history. It shows what can happen if one dreams about possibilities and doesn't accept conventional thinking.

HOW YOU CAN DO IT TOO

You can apply the principle of robust design by following these steps:
1. Don't accept conditions that are less than desirable. Resolve to try to find a better way.
2. Don't accept the first thing that comes to your mind when you are trying to improve the condition.
3. Brainstorm with yourself or with others to find alternatives to improve the condition.
4. Do "out-of-the-box" thinking to develop creative alternatives to the current situation. Do not discard alternatives that may appear to be crazy.
5. Consider all the ideas and then select the one that seems best.

—Weimerskirch—

Innovation in the workplace

THE STORY

THE CAPTAIN AND THE ELEPHANT

One of the applicants for the United States Government's President's Award was the Naval Aviation Depot at Norfolk, Virginia. Their mission is to serve as a technical maintenance arm for ships, aircraft, and missiles. When President Reagan privatized these maintenance activities, the Naval Aviation Depot had to compete with industrial companies, in order to get these maintenance contracts.

They had done some amazing things to improve their performance. As a result, they were able to refurbish fighter jets at a significantly lower cost than their private competitors. For this, they were nominated for the President's Award. I was the leader of the site visit team assigned to validate their performance.

The Naval Aviation Depot was commanded by a Navy Captain, Captain Tom. I interviewed him and asked him to describe his leadership style.

He said "OK, you have asked me for the time, and I am going to tell you how to build a watch." He went on to explain his belief that a leader can get the most out of people by inspiring them to reach their full potential. A leader does that by energizing employees by putting meaning into their jobs. That style of leadership, he explained, was largely responsible for the outstanding performance of the Naval Aviation Depot.

One particular incident especially impressed me. One of the jobs on the base was to keep it looking neat and clean. There would be cigarette butts and leaves around the buildings that needed to be cleaned up. Everybody hated that job and Captain Tom had to all but pull teeth to get people to do it.

Finally, he got tired of having to cajole people to do this undesirable job, so he invented the "elephant." He took a regular commercial floor sweeper and fitted it with a large vacuum tube that could be controlled from the driver's seat. It was a giant vacuum cleaner but looked a little bit like an elephant with its long trunk.

Suddenly, it became fun to keep the base clean. Everybody wanted to drive the elephant and go

around sucking up the debris. A job that had been pure drudgery now became one that was exciting. Innovation in the workplace can put meaning in ordinary jobs.

Source: Freestockphotos.biz

WHAT WAS THE PROCESS OF DISCOVERY?

The relationship between employees and their employer has evolved over the years. In the early years of my career, the management style was one of command and control. Employees were looked upon as commodities to be used as management saw fit. Management issued the orders from on high and the employees were expected to carry them out. "Management by Objectives" was the mantra of the times. Management set the objectives and employees were expected to figure out how to meet them. Managers believed their job was to "motivate" the workers on the premise that employees would not motivate themselves.

Gradually, the terms "employee participation" and "participative management" came into use. That concept was that employees could contribute valuable ideas to improve productivity. Self-directed work teams were used to give employees a greater role in decision-making. It was now management's job to get employees more involved in the way work was performed.

The quality movement of the mid-1980's introduced the idea that management's job is to solve systems problems. The late quality expert, W. Edwards Deming, stated that 85% of problems occurring in an organization are the result of system's problems. That is, the problems are not caused by employees themselves, but rather by unclear instructions as the work flows from one operation to the next. These problems are beyond the control of individual workers. Only management can fix them. Under this concept, managers are there to serve the workers, not the other way around. The result was a much more pleasant work environment.

Now, in the 21st century, the concept of "Employee Wellness" has emerged. In this digital age, the divide between the employee's work life and personal life has blurred. The pervasiveness of e-mails, texts, and social media means that employees are available virtually any time of the day. They can no longer just put in their workday and then disengage. They are on duty 24 hours a day. This creates a very stressful environment.

Companies are recognizing this and responding with Employee Wellness programs. Employee Wellness programs are based on the fact that employees are human beings with emotions and the need for fulfillment. They are a valuable human capital resource. Employee Wellness programs go beyond the work environment and encompass the physical, emotional and social health of every employee in all aspects of their life. The objective is to improve employee productivity.

LESSONS LEARNED

Employees are an organization's most important resource -- more important than financial or physical resources. Employees who have emotional or social challenges cannot be productive at work. Employee well-being is, therefore, an important part of any company's human capital management strategy.

We can take a lesson from Captain Tom, mentioned above, when he said that it is important to inspire people to realize their full potential. This involves several factors. First of all, employees must understand the mission of the organization and their role in accomplishing that mission. Job stress is reduced when employees understand why they and their jobs are important.

People's jobs are an important part of their socialization. Compatible work associates are a large part of job satisfaction. They celebrate achievements together and they support each other when they have a bad day at the office.

Finally, job stress is reduced when employees believe they have the opportunity for advancement. The opportunity for advancement allows them to realize their full potential.

So, do Employee Wellness programs pay off? Numerous studies show that healthy employees are almost twice as productive as those who are not.

Retention rates are also improved, thereby reducing recruitment and training costs.

Howard Schultz, Chairman of Starbucks

People want guidance, not rhetoric; they need to know what the plan of action is and how it will be implemented. They want to be given responsibility to help solve the problem and the authority to act on it.

At the bottom line, evidence shows that the stock price of those companies named as "Best Places to Work" significantly outperforms the S&P 500. Several studies show this. Results reported vary somewhat depending upon the method of calculation.

This chart shows an example; the stock price of "Best Places to Work" outperformed the S&P 500 by 82% (or 1.8 times) over an 11-year period from 2009 through 2019.

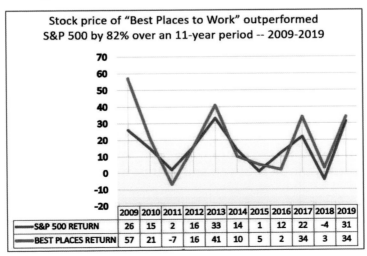

Stock price of "Best Places to Work" outperformed S&P 500 by 82% over an 11-year period -- 2009-2019

	2009	2010	2011	2012	2013	2014	2015	2016	2017	2018	2019
S&P 500 RETURN	26	15	2	16	33	14	1	12	22	-4	31
BEST PLACES RETURN	57	21	-7	16	41	10	5	2	34	3	34

HOW YOU CAN DO IT TOO

The key to job fulfillment is to focus not on **how** the work is performed, but rather on **why** the work is performed. When I get on the treadmill each morning, I dread the half hour of walking at a brisk pace and going nowhere. It is not a pleasant task. But then I stop to think of the reason I do it. Exercise is important to maintain my health. That makes the job tolerable if not enjoyable.

Or consider another example. If my job were to move pieces of paper one piece at a time from one stack to another, it would be considered the most boring job in the world. But if those pieces of paper were dollar bills and I got to keep every bill I placed on the new pile, it would be the most exciting job in the world. Both jobs are the same, but now I understand <u>why</u> I am doing it.

So, whatever your job is, think about <u>why</u> that job is important and how it contributes to the organization's objectives. Think about ways to improve the job and make it more challenging. And get the right balance between your work life and your life outside of work.

If you supervise employees, help them understand <u>why</u> their job is important. Explain the mission of the organization and their role in achieving that mission. Help them see the big picture and show them how they can help the organization improve. Inspire them to realize their full potential.

—Weimerskirch—

Chapter 09
Working in an organization

📖 Making things happen

THE STORY

In 1988, my job at Honeywell was rather tenuous. Honeywell, like many companies, was "right sizing." My position on the corporate staff was vulnerable. It was a stressful time for me. I was 52 at the time: too young to retire but too old to be very attractive in the labor market. A consultant friend of mine suggested that I volunteer to be an examiner for the newly formed Malcolm Baldrige National Quality Award Program. It would look good on my résumé in case I had to look for another job. The Program featured a public sector/private sector partnership aimed at getting broad participation to achieve a cost-effective operation. They were looking for volunteers, so I signed on as an examiner in 1989.

I found personal success and enthusiasm in the Baldrige Program. I was soon promoted to senior examiner, then judge and then Chairman of the Panel of Judges. I used my experience in the Baldrige Program to install a successful quality program at Honeywell. That got my career on track again and eventually I was promoted to Corporate Vice President of Quality.

WHAT WAS THE PROCESS OF DISCOVERY?

The Malcolm Baldrige National Quality Award
Program (now called the Malcolm Baldrige
Performance Excellence Program) was formed by a
resolution of Congress and signed into law by
President Ronald Reagan in 1987. It was instituted
to improve the competitiveness of U.S. industry that
was under serious international threat at the time.

Malcolm Baldrige Award
Source: Wikimedia Commons

The Baldrige Program had an immediate,
revolutionary impact. At the 1992 Award ceremony,
then Commerce Secretary Barbara Hackman

Franklin said, "The Baldrige Program has revolutionized the way in which U.S. companies are managed."

Over the years, the program was expanded to include Health Care, Education, Government, and Non-profit organizations. Now, thousands of organizations use the criteria as their primary vehicle for driving improvement.

The Baldrige criteria consists of a series of deep, penetrating questions about how an organization works. Questions like:

- What are your organization's mission, vision, and values?
- How is your vision translated into measurable plans and goals?
- What are your organization's sustainable competitive advantages?
- How do your sustainable competitive advantages align with your customers' requirements and expectations?
- In what way do your key processes add value for your customers?
- How does your employee selection process relate to your business objectives?
- How do your results compare with world-class benchmarks?

As Baldrige examiners, we were required to take an intensive, three-day training program. I was immediately impressed with the power of the award process. For me, the Baldrige criteria represented a complete management system. Over the years, I had struggled with the various quality concepts and tried to fit them all together with limited success. The Baldrige criteria put them all together for me. At the end of the first day of training, each student was asked to comment about how the day had gone for them. I stood up and said, "I just learned more in one day than in the previous 29 years."

LESSONS LEARNED:

It is important to think of an organization as a system. A system has the necessary components, all in the right relationship with each other. Systems thinking is critical to an organization's long-term success.

> The Chief Executive Officer (CEO) of a large corporation once said, "I feel like I am at the wheel of a big ship. I turn the wheel but sometimes I'm not sure if the wheel is connected to anything. I don't know if I am steering the ship or not." Obviously, running a large company is a challenging assignment, but it is not impossible. It is necessary to view a company as a "system." That means that all the necessary components are in place and in the proper relationship to each other. The concept of a company (or any organization) as a system was a rather elusive idea until the advent of the Malcolm Baldrige National Quality Award Program in 1987. The Baldrige criteria connects the wheel to the rudder of the ship so that leaders can steer it.

Source: vecteezy.com

So, what does a complete management system look like? A management system has seven components and they have a sequential relationship with each other. I diagram it this way.

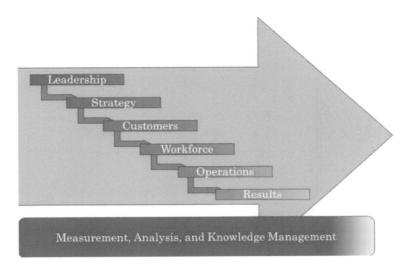

Leadership: Effective leadership is a matter of articulating clear mission, vision, and values statements for the organization and then setting breakthrough expectations. There is a distinction between leadership and management. Leaders take organizations to heights never seen before. Managers work the process as it exists.

Strategic Planning: Strategic plans translate the organization's mission, vision, and values statements into measurable objectives and goals. They also specify how the objectives and goals are to be accomplished.

Customer: All organizations exist to create value for their customers. That requires an understanding of customer requirements and expectations and well-defined processes for delivering customer value.

Workforce: An organization's workforce must be inspired and empowered to perform their jobs to the best of their ability. To do this, employees must be trained to have the skills, knowledge, and abilities to capably implement their processes.

Operations: Processes shape how an organization performs its work. They define the day-to- day procedures all employees follow in carrying out their jobs.

Results: Results measure the degree to which the organization's goals and objectives have been met. There should be results for all stakeholders including the impact on society.

Measurement, Analysis, and Knowledge Management: Organizations must be managed with evidence based, factual knowledge that enables disciplined analysis and correct decisions.

HOW YOU CAN DO IT TOO

The concepts of the Baldrige criteria can be applied to any organization no matter how small. They can even be applied at an individual level.

The key is SYSTEMS THINKING.

In any situation, it is helpful to think about all the parts that must be in place and how they all fit together. Anyone can benefit from the introspective thinking that comes from using the Baldrige criteria. A copy of the criteria can be downloaded from the Baldrige web site on the internet. Many companies have submitted applications since 1988. But millions of criteria booklets have been purchased and downloaded to guide companies trying to improve but not yet interested in applying for the award.

John Ruskin, British philosopher

Source: Commons.wikimedia.org

—Weimerskirch—

People manage what you measure

THE STORY

When I was vice president of quality at a large, national bank I often started my day by visiting branch offices and similar

> **People Inside Your Organization Manage What _You_ Measure**

sites to see what was actually happening as people did their work, not just read about it in reports.

Sometimes this meant watching processes that people had already earmarked as potential improvement projects, and other times meant watching processes where I hadn't personally worked and didn't know in detail. On a beautiful morning, with that sunrise light still low enough to make long shadows and send shafts of sunlight to directly illuminate the classic murals on the bank's walls, an enthusiastic, slightly impatient crowd was forming.

Only a very few customers walked over to the long row of traditional teller positions; only a few positions were open there because it was still so early in the morning. If you watched those few customers, you saw them exchange friendly greetings with the teller, heard a little banter about the beautiful weather, and after a quick deposit or dropping-off a loan form or signature card, the customer left with a "see you later" and a wave. A typical interaction with a typical retail consumer customer.

At the end of the long row of mostly empty teller positions was another, very short row of tellers, set at a right angle to the longer row. This other teller row was nearly hidden in the corner and you'd be unlikely to see it if you just walked into the bank.

All of the short-row teller positions were open -- but a line was forming. The line was made from small business and shop owners who were making deposits from yesterday's business and receiving bags of coins and paper bills to make change for cash-paying customers today at their shop.

Things seemed to be going well, but one shop owner at the end of a line looked to his left, then his right, then to his watch, and then back at his line.

Finally, his patience exhausted, he left that commercial customer line and walked over to the retail tellers in the long row of teller positions. She was idle, waiting for a retail bank customer – a type that was rare at this early hour.

He said "Hi."

She said "Hi" with a big smile.

He handed her a canvas bag with checks, paper bills, coins, and deposit slips. And he also gave her a list of the coinage and bills he would need that day for making change with customers of his business.

She looked at it and then looked at him and said with sincere disappointment, "I'm sorry. I can't help you with this. You have to go back to the commercial tellers."

"Why can't you help me? You have no other customers at your window. You can take deposits. And you can make change. Why do I need to go back to the commercial teller line?"

Her reply was sincere and smiling, but it left him speechless for a minute.

"Well, you see, customer satisfaction is our number one goal. And we've learned that the amount of time it takes us to process a customer request is directly tied to how satisfied our customer will be. The shorter the time the happier the customer."

She smiled and continued. "So, they put a new measure in place for all of the retail tellers. It measures the time from when I start your transaction to when I finish. I'm a retail teller."

"Your transaction will take me much longer than a traditional, retail transaction. I will need to make the deposits and gather up the right amount of coins and bills for you to make daily change at your store. Then, when I'm done, I'll close the transaction. But by then my average time is way longer than it should be for retail tellers and I'll have to work super-fast the rest of the day to bring down my average time per customer."

"You see, commercial tellers are expected to take longer than retail tellers, so they can do what you need without being penalized. I'd like to take your deposits and get you your change, but it will make my numbers look awful!"

He smiled. And said he was going up to the CEO's office to ask about this new measure.

WHAT WAS THE PROCESS OF DISCOVERY?

The moral is: what you measure is what you manage.

Retail tellers were expected to handle regular customers' requests in a very short length of time. Quick transactions. The retail teller knew that her average time per transaction was a proxy for how well she is doing her job. Faster transactions equals happier customers. She knew what the bank measured and she therefore knew what **she** must manage.

Shortly after the merchant shared his unhappiness with the CEO, the measure of average transaction time was refined. Two, separate measures replaced the old measure. One new measure was the average transaction time for **retail** customers, and the other new measure, the average transaction time for **commercial transactions**.

The teller knew that merchant expectations were much different than retail customers. But the teller was afraid to act as a commercial teller if the measures were going to evaluate her performance against the retail standard. She knew that merchant satisfaction was important, but his unhappiness or happiness would not be reflected in the retail transaction time metric—his happiness wouldn't be on any metrics. But her longer, average cycle time would be on the meter evaluating her performance.

LESSONS LEARNED:

Source: Wikimedia Commons

1.   People working *in the process* are not allowed to change the process. For that, they need management's approval and the time and resources to make such a process change happen.

2. Management unintentionally changed the commercial transaction process by changing the measure. They should have measured the impact of the new measurement to identify any unintended consequence of having retail customers idle at their station ⁓ while commercial customers had to wait in line for their

commercial teller. Much of what you discover in Gemba walks is **"Obvious, after the fact."**

HOW YOU CAN DO IT TOO

Are people in your organization empowered? Go to the Gemba to find out.

Consider each process your organization provides them to do their job. *An empowered person is one who has the means to deliver what their customers expect of them.* If customers expect something that the employee can only provide by extraordinary means or by going around the process, that employee is unlikely to do what the customer expects.

Gemba Walks

I didn't have a name for it in 1993, I just thought of it as *Management by Walking Around*. But in the world of Lean and Six Sigma, we'd call it a *Gemba Walk* – go to where the work is being done and watch.

Don't interrupt and don't interfere.

When you understand what is happening, then you can ask what, why, when, and discuss with those doing the job about how it might be designed differently to get better results and lower costs.

"Genba (also romanized as gemba) is a Japanese term meaning "the actual place". Japanese detectives call the crime scene genba, and Japanese TV reporters may refer to themselves as reporting from genba. In business, genba refers to the place where value is created; in manufacturing the genba is the factory floor. It can be any "site" such as a construction site, sales floor or where the service provider interacts directly with the customer." https://en.wikipedia.org/wiki/Gemba

A Gemba walk lets managers see the actual work process, observe employees, understand the work process see opportunities for improvement (OFI).

—Fechter—

📖 A brief history of quality

THE STORY

My career began as a quality engineer with Honeywell, Inc in 1960. At that time, the common believe was that quality costs money. The better the quality, the higher the cost. Many times, I would hear my older colleagues say, "Let's not give the customer a Cadillac when they are paying for a Chevrolet."

We would think in terms of "Acceptable Quality Levels." Good enough was good enough. Better than the acceptable quality level would cost too much. Quality was regarded as inspection at the end of the line. So, Americans became accustomed to marginal quality and shoddy products. We can recall cars that didn't run and household appliances that didn't work.

But then the Japanese economy started to recover after World War II. Japan brought in American quality experts like Dr. W. Edwards Deming and Dr. Joseph Juran. They had a major challenge in front of them.

In those days "Made in Japan" was synonymous with junk. But the Japanese learned their lesson well. Gradually, products made in Japan were superior to those made in the USA. First, the Japanese threatened our automobile industry with their reliable products. Next came television and electronic products. U.S industry was in dire straits. There was a national emergency. Suddenly, quality became a competitive necessity.

That competitive threat was met with the institution of the Malcolm Baldrige National Quality Program.

Signed into law by President Reagan in 1987, it made quality a national priority. Finally, we came to realize that high quality products cost less, not more, than shoddy ones. It only made sense. Doing things right the first time eliminates waste and drives costs down.

WHAT WAS THE PROCESS OF DISCOVERY?

My understanding of "quality" evolved over the years. Gradually, I realized that it is a broader concept than I had at first thought. Initially, I viewed quality as a topic that pertained to production processes. That is where the product is built and therefore quality products seemed to be the end objective.

I had not yet comprehended the concept of "Performance Excellence" which encompasses everything that an organization does.

As I learned more and more about quality, I realized that it was my job to teach others, particularly management, about quality as well. Since the printed word is an effective way to communicate, I developed several booklets explaining the concepts:

1. The Quality Improvement Owner's Manual

This booklet was intended to make people aware of quality concepts. It was first published in 1988 before those concepts were really understood. At that time, quality was an elusive, rather intangible, concept that was having no real impact on Honeywell's operations.

2. Quality is a Work in Progress

This booklet, intended to be inspirational, used pictures like this one to communicate the idea that leaders need to have a vision of greatness and to set breakthrough expectations.

3. Baldrige for the Baffled.

Baldrige for the Baffled put the Baldrige criteria into a language that would communicate with senior management. The Baldrige Quality criteria (now Performance Excellence criteria) represent a comprehensive, holistic definition of quality. It is structured in the form of questions that an organization should ask itself (and answer) if it aspires to be a great organization. I call it "The Large Open Book Test" of everything you should ask yourself but never took time to do it.

But, while the criteria are comprehensive, they are not the easiest thing to understand. Someone once described it as two PhD's talking to each other. I had to find a way to put it into more common, everyday language. We called it "The Baldrige criteria not quite by the book." We tried to use language that is used every day in business.

Another aspect of my endeavor to educate was to show how an organization might answer the questions. That is: What are some of the practices that the really great organizations employ in running their business? As stated previously, the Baldrige criteria ask the questions. Organizations still have to find the answers. The practices discussed in Baldrige for the Baffled represented the state-of-the-art thinking of performance excellence at the time.

4. Total Quality Management: Strategies and Techniques Proven at Today's Most Successful Companies

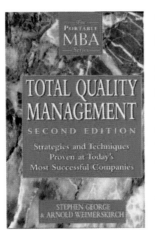

This book was written with my colleague, Steve George.

Initially, my idea was to invent a hypothetical company that would get a perfect score against the Baldrige criteria – the perfect company. Steve felt that would be too theoretical and would not get much traction in the business marketplace. He countered with the idea that we should find real companies that were best at various management practices. We identified over 50 companies and wrote about what those companies actually did. The book has been a huge success, selling more than 30,000 copies.

LESSONS LEARNED:

The concept of "quality" has evolved over time. Its scope has expanded to encompass all work done in all kinds of organizations. It continues to evolve so that it always reflects the leading edge of validated management practice.

In addition to deciding on the Baldrige winners, one of the other jobs of the Baldrige judges was to lead the annual process to improve the Baldrige criteria. Since I was Chairman of the Panel of Judges, I played a key role in this process.

At one of our meetings, I stated that the Baldrige criteria should represent the "leading edge of validated management practice." Management theory is continually advancing. There are always experts who are doing research to learn new things. Some of the new knowledge is valuable. Others are just a fad with no real underlying content. There is a book entitled <u>Fad Surfing in the Boardroom</u> authored by Eileen C. Shapiro.

> The book defines Fad Surfing as:
> "Fad Surfing (n): the practice of riding the crest of the latest management panacea and then paddling out again in time to ride the next one; always absorbing for managers and lucrative for consultants; frequently disastrous for organizations."

Since new management theories are almost always developed by experts, there is a tendency for management to employ those theories without really understanding them. The result is that the theories fail to live up to expectations and the initiative ends in failure. This probably explains why up to 85% of performance improvement initiatives fail.

So, my recommendation was that the Baldrige criteria should incorporate new management theories only after they had been validated in practice. On the other hand, we should stay on the forefront of those theories once they are validated. We should then incorporate them into the criteria as soon as possible so that the criteria are always on the "leading edge of validated management practice." Even though I articulated that concept in 1993, it is still used today as the mantra for the evolution of the Baldrige criteria.

One of my primary learnings from the Baldrige criteria was the concept of "management processes." As mentioned previously, I had originally thought of processes in the context of production process (i.e. in the factory where the product is manufactured). But the I came to realize that all work can be defined as a process. The way in which the Finance Department does its accounting work is a process. The way in which a company does its strategic planning is a process. All work is a process. Once I learned this, I was able to get this concept incorporated into the Baldrige criteria. We called the concept "management processes." Over time, as the concept was accepted, the Baldrige Program changed the name from "quality criteria" to "performance excellence criteria."

HOW YOU CAN DO IT TOO

You too can take the Baldrige "Large Open Book Test" at an individual level. Regardless of the organization you work for or your position in it, it will be beneficial to look at the questions contained in the criteria. There are Baldrige criteria for Education, Health Care and Non-profits as well as Business. So, there are always criteria to fit your environment. Copies can be obtained from the Baldrige web site. You will find it to be a mind-expanding experience.

—Weimerskirch—

10 principles of change

THE STORY

By 1997, the Quality Program that I had implemented as Honeywell's Vice President of Quality had matured to the point that it was achieving amazing results. We called it the "Honeywell Quality Value" to communicate that we wanted quality thinking to be an intrinsic value in everything we did at Honeywell.

We started the program in 1990 and by 1997 our sales were up sharply, and all of our financial indicators were showing dramatic improvement. Honeywell management attributed this largely to the Honeywell Quality Value Program.

About this time, Honeywell had collected a group of young, high talent people, visualized as the next leaders of the corporation. They were having a series of meetings to talk about how they could develop their potential and have the greatest impact on the company. So, they called me up and said your Quality Program is the best thing Honeywell has ever done, so would you come and explain what it is you did? I had a reputation as a change agent. They invited me to spend a day with them and lead a workshop. I had about two weeks to prepare.

WHAT WAS THE PROCESS OF DISCOVERY?

While I had a broad strategy in place, I had never consciously thought, in detail, about how I had approached the development of the Honeywell Quality Value Program. I sat down and brainstormed with myself and listed 25 things I had done. Then I thought, no guru can have 25 points, so I boiled it down to 10 points. I stated a principle and embellished it with quotes. To me, eloquent quotes add meaning and depth to any point I am trying to make.

> I called my presentation "The Flight of a Corporate Seagull" in reference to the euphemism about corporate staff.
>
> *We fly in, eat your food, make a big mess and then we fly out again. Yet, you can't shoot us because we are a protected species.*

In my presentation, I described the process I used to get the Honeywell Quality Value implemented and the challenges I met along the way. Then I went into the 10 Principles of Change that I used to lead the quality movement at Honeywell.

LESSONS LEARNED:

Everyone should develop their own leadership style regardless of their position in the organization. This gives clarity to your job, makes you more effective, and helps meet your objectives.

Here are the 10 principles of my leadership style in leading the quality program at Honeywell:

10 PRINCIPLES OF CHANGE

#1   Talk the walk

> *"If I have seen further it is by standing upon the shoulders of giants"*   Sir Isaac Newton

I visualized I was standing on the shoulders of the COO and CEO, getting into their minds and supporting their leadership style.   So often you hear, 'you've got to convince the boss to do things differently.' That's a fool's errand. Every CEO wants to lead a great company; no CEO wants to lead their company into demise. Talk the walk.

#2   Use a credible management model

"Everything should be as simple as possible and not one bit simpler" Albert Einstein

Most people are willing to accept a credible standard, so don't waste time inventing one of your own. And keep it simple. Even the most intelligent people will not take the time to understand complex concepts. The Malcolm Baldrige Performance Excellence framework was the credible management model that worked for me.

#3   Stay focused

"I go where the puck is going to be." Wayne Gretzky

You will meet obstacles in making change, so stay focused and look ahead to see what your next actions will be. Don't let setbacks get you down. I always imagined that I was playing in a hockey game. I might get checked into the boards, but the puck is still out there. I picked myself up and went after it.

#4   Recognize and correct mistakes early

"Perseverance is not a long race; it is many short races one after another" Walter Elliott

Mistakes are inevitable. No one can accurately predict the future. When you make a mistake, learn from it and keep moving.

#5   Get horizontal

"In the years ahead, corporations will sort themselves out into those that can compete on the playing field of global business and those that either sell out or fail.

Winning will require the kind of skill, speed and dexterity that can only come from an emotionally energized workforce" Noel Tichey

Change agents do not necessarily appear on an organizational chart. Find the people who want to make change regardless of where they are in the organization. Then empower them to make change happen.

In my work at Honeywell, I formed what I called my "Network of Champions." I invited people from all parts of the Honeywell Corporation to work with me to achieve the quality revolution. They didn't report to me. They stayed in their jobs. But I expected them to go over and above their assigned jobs to help implement the quality program. I was amazed at the dedicated people from all departments and all levels of the organization who volunteered.

#6   Use the carrot and the stick
"You can get more with kind words and a gun than you can with kind words alone"
Willie Sutton, Bank Robber

Positive behavior needs to be rewarded and negative behavior needs to have consequences. Don't let the "nay sayers" influence your thinking.

#7   Train, train, train

"If the only tool you have is a hammer, you tend to see everything as a nail"
Abraham Maslow

People cannot do what they do not know how to do. Knowledge is a powerful vehicle for making change happen.

#8   Reward the desired behavior

> *"Water what you want to grow"*
> Spencer W. Kimball

You can change behavior on a dime if you reward the desired behavior.

#9   Measure cause/effect improvement

> *"If we would first know where we are and whither we are tending, we could better judge what to do and how to do it"*
> Abraham Lincoln

You can't manage what you don't measure. The best measures relate to daily activities. Measures should be used to predict the future.

#10   Drive for results

> *"There are two kinds of companies in the world today. The quick and the dead."*
> Andrew Grove, Intel

The longer a project takes, the more likely it is to fail. People will miss a deadline by the amount of time they are given to make it.

I stated these principles 20 years ago. Most of the people quoted here have faded into history. Yet their messages are timeless. For me, they are still appropriate today. I still use these principles in my everyday life.

HOW YOU CAN DO IT TOO

Everyone is a change agent or should be.

Regardless of your job in the organization, you are a change agent. If your job is frustrating, you should work to remove those frustrations by making changes. If your job is challenging, you should make changes to have a greater impact on the organization.

Analyze your environment and your leadership style. Don't let yourself be the victim of circumstances. Develop a set of principles that you can use to make changes to your job and your organization. Your principles will be different from mine because I worked in a different environment. Your principles will have to match you own environment. They will give clarity to your job and help you meet your objectives. You will find your job to be more rewarding and your career will prosper.

—Weimerskirch—

Mortgaging the factory

THE STORY

For decades, a popular management tactic called *Management by Walking Around* (**MBWA**) put a revealing spotlight on what's actually happening on the factory floor versus what the regular reports and summaries say is happening. A contemporary term for this approach is called *Going to the Gemba* to see first-hand what's happening.

Both approaches – MBWA and Going to the Gemba -- are fact-filled approaches. At first, to those just watching and not working within the observed processes, things look busy, active, and normal. Materials move from line to line, boxes are filled, boxes are emptied, forms are filled-out, and data are entered into work screens.

And here, after focused watching, a new character jumps on the shoulder of those who have come to the *Gemba* or are *Managing by Walking Around*. This character is named WHY.

It's plain to see what's happening. But WHY puts a special filter on the scene. Does it need to happen the way it is happening? Does it need to happen at all?

For example, it is Saturday morning and most lines are idle, with only a few, partial crews at work. But this line I'm watching on this Saturday is working a full speed, almost urgently. After a new batch of products is boxed, team members walk quickly to the supervisor to check the numbers being tallied and what work in process has yet to be finished.
Compared to regular production activity seen during

my MBWA weekday observations, this Saturday crew's behavior seems different.

WHY?

Keep watching. Few team members are checking the wall clock. Instead, most are checking the pile of empty boxes and the growing pile of packed boxes.

WHY?

Leaving the production line, I go to the planner's office to see what the plan vs. actual inventory is for this line – the line I've been watching this Saturday. They closed production Friday afternoon showing 100% on track – planned production was equal to finished goods inventory on the factory floor and ready for shipment.

So WHY are they making so much product this Saturday?

A walk through the finished goods inventory gives the answer. The numbers submitted to factory inventory systems on Friday afternoon reported that everything scheduled to be built was built and was available to ship from finished goods inventory on Monday.

That's not what I saw.

I saw a lot of empty shelves when walking through the finished goods area. It turns out that production created a "mortgage" on Friday, reporting that more finished goods were built than were actually built.

Numbers submitted on Friday were not true. That "mortgage" of missing, finished goods had to be paid before Monday. So, the crew was called in for mandatory overtime on Saturday to finish what was not completed by Friday afternoon.

Employees used the weekend to finish the job on Saturday, so that all "reported finished" products would be available to ship from finished goods inventory on Monday.

WHAT WAS THE PROCESS OF DISCOVERY?

Going to the Gemba – to where the work is actually done – is a rich opportunity to see what is really happening. By frequently visiting the Gemba during the regular work week, I had learned what was "normal" process flow, normal behavior, and typical hiccups.

A Gemba Walk?

"Gemba" means "the real place" in Japanese. The Gemba is where the real work happens.

Three rules"

1. **Go and See.**
2. **Ask why.**
3. **Respect the people.** Focus on finding process weaknesses, not people weaknesses.

I understood WHY things were being done.

Visiting on Saturday showed unusual, different behavior than I was familiar with Monday-Friday. People on Saturday were focusing on empty boxes to fill rather than clock-watching. There was an air of urgency and frequent checks of production tallies. A new WHY entered my mind.

This was before the sophistication and process controls of *Just in Time* inventory. In that era, normal behavior during the week showed full shelves of finished goods inventory. But this weekend there were empty spaces on Saturday that the crew was working hard to fill.

> "We get brilliant results from average people managing brilliant processes - while our competitors get average or worse results from brilliant people managing broken processes"
>
> Fujio Cho, honorary chairman of Toyota Motor Corporation.

First issue: the actual cost of the finished goods for this production line was higher than budgeted because personnel were paid for a full shift on Friday and also paid for an overtime shift on Saturday. This meant that the Cost of Goods Sold would be higher than budgets had planned for and that profits would slip. Or, if personnel were not paid for the Saturday overtime, then morale would decline, and turnover would increase -- driving personnel to leave the unfair situation.

Second issue: If the process used to make product regularly takes more production hours than assumed in the standards, then the plan-actual finished goods discrepancy would grow without mortgage-paying Saturday overtime – maybe some Sunday overtime would also be needed if sales volumes go up?

WHY do the process capability numbers indicate less time is required than is truly required?

WHY have line supervisors historically used *mortgaging* to fill the gap instead of reporting that the standards were inaccurate? WHY hasn't line management exposed the problem and asked management and process engineers to help fix the system -- so actual hours needed are properly reflected in the standard?

A **core issue** was probably the environment and expectations created by management. Was it safe for people to report when processes and systems needed fixing? Or, had management made it a career-limiting move to report that a process was unable to deliver the volumes expected?

LESSONS LEARNED:

Asking WHY on Saturday led to my discovery that the management culture in place made it very hard to raise one's hand and tell management something was wrong. Employees did not feel empowered to communicate all the facts.

The crew working Monday-Friday on this line was not lazy, not suffering from sabotage, nor high absenteeism. Rather, the work simply couldn't be completed in the time allotted.

People were forced to come in during weekends and the department paid overtime rates. Mortgaging was improper and not ethical because it made the records incomplete or false. But until the culture of "raise no issues" changed, mortgaging persisted.

HOW YOU CAN DO IT TOO

Use MBWA and Go to the Gemba.

Not just once.
- Go often enough to know normal from not normal.
- Watch.
- Learn what is happening.
- Only then, ask WHY – **the reason to ask is to understand, not to berate or challenge or criticize.**

Sabotage by people in any work environment is extremely rare. If plan is not equal to actual, watch, then ask WHY?

And make it safe for people to tell you the truth so they don't need to take out a "mortgage" to give you the numbers you expect, not the honest numbers showing what the process is really delivering.

—Fechter—

Customer delight

THE STORY

The license plates on the Honeywell CEO's car read "Delight em." He wanted his signature legacy to be that Honeywell would delight its customers. Which is to say that we would exceed customer's expectations. Nowadays we hear the term "exceeding expectations" quite frequently. It has become a cliché. But in the mid-1990's, it was a relatively new term. But how does a company achieve customer delight? It is more than just an inspirational message. There is a science behind it.

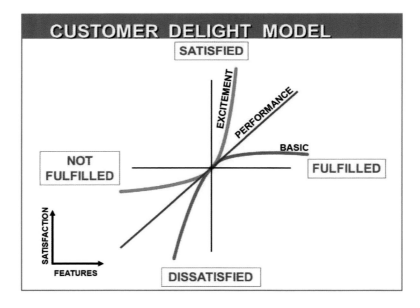

The concept of "customer delight" was developed by Dr. Noriaki Kano, a professor at Tokyo Rika University. He portrayed the concept as shown in this diagram.

The chart plots the degree to which customer expectations are fulfilled or not fulfilled plotted against the degree of customer satisfaction or dissatisfaction. Customer expectations encompass the entire relationship with the customer including the product or service, but also all of the other factors that go into the transaction.

Some examples will help explain:
- **Basic features** are ones that the customer expects to be fulfilled. You expect the brakes on your automobile to work. If they work, that is simply meeting your expectation. There is no chance to get you excited. If they do not work, you will become dissatisfied in a hurry.
- **Performance features** are ones where the customer will be increasingly more satisfied the better the performance. The smoothness of the ride in your automobile is an example. The smoother the ride, the more satisfied you will be with the automobile.
- **Excitement features** are ones that the customers didn't expect and are delighted when they find them. At one time, the placement of coffee cup holders in your car was an excitement feature because you didn't expect to find a convenient place to put your coffee cup while driving. That quickly became a basic feature once every car had them.
- **Excitement features quickly become basic or expected features.** Nowadays, excitement features tend to be related to the relationship with the customer. Extra friendly service still tends to be an excitement feature since it is not very common or consistent.

My favorite customer delight story came from our Miami office. That office had a very disciplined procedure for dispatching service technicians to go out and service Honeywell installed equipment. The skill of the technicians was matched with the complexity of the job. Routes were planned to minimize travel time and maximize technician's time on service job. Customer responsiveness was top priority. When a customer called, they had to be serviced.

The man in charge of dispatching technicians was a very competent and dedicated employee, but he had some Yogi Berra characteristics. Yogi Berra was the famous New York Yankee baseball player. He was very skillful but he had a habit of doing some unusual things and saying some silly things. One of those was "When you come to a fork in the road, take it." This technician was somewhat like that. One day, he complained that computers don't work. His office mate pointed that that was because he was trying to use his hand-held calculator as his mouse. This background is important to the rest of the story.

On one particularly busy day, all of the technicians, including all of the supervisors, had been dispatched into the field. There was simply no one available. But then a customer called needing his equipment serviced on an emergency basis. The dispatcher was not trained to do equipment maintenance, but he knew he had to respond. So, he put on his Honeywell cap and jacket, got in his car and drove to the customer's plant. The problem was with a security camera; the dispatcher asked for a ladder. He climbed up the ladder, screwed off the lens cap, blew on it and screwed it back on. The system worked perfectly and he was a hero.

After several weeks, that same customer called with another service request. The dispatcher said he would get a technician out there immediately. The customer said "we don't want just any technician. We want the one who came out last time." Now the dispatcher was in a bind. He did not know the equipment. What was he going to do now?

He was a quick thinker. He had an experienced technician accompany him on the call. When he got to the customer's plant, he explained that he was training a new technician and had brought him along so he could see how the work is done. The experienced technician quickly fixed the problem and the dispatcher was still a hero.

WHAT WAS THE PROCESS OF DISCOVERY?

One day in a staff meeting, I commented that for a company that wants to delight its customers, fully half of our company had no idea what our customers think of us.

We didn't measure customer satisfaction. So, I suggested that we require every business unit to measure customer satisfaction with the aspiration that we exceed our customers' expectations and delight them. I was given control of 5% of our executive bonus program to make this happen.

That was an interesting experience. I travelled extensively throughout the company explaining the various methods for measuring customer satisfaction and the options that were open to them. I also explained the requirements for earning their 5% bonus. Simple as the task was, learning was slow. One business unit even discarded any data from dissatisfied customers on the premise that those customers were not objective. But gradually, the concept caught on and our business units started to measure customer satisfaction and Honeywell was striving to delight its customers.

LESSONS LEARNED:

Customer satisfaction has several dimensions. Relationships and brand recognition are equally as important as the price and the product or service offered. Customers are loyal when their expectations are exceeded.

Customer satisfaction (or customer delight) is based on four factors that customers value:
1. The quality of the product or services that the company provides
2. The relationship that the company develops with its customers

3. The price that the company charges its customers
4. The company's brand, which is really an indication of how much customers trust the company.

All of these factors must be compared to the performance of competitors. Not always easy to do but very important.

It is interesting to note that customer relationships and brand play a very big role in forming the customer's perception of value.

HOW YOU CAN DO IT TOO

Anyone working in business, education, health care or non-profit organizations can use the concepts of the Customer Delight Model. Thinking through the basic, performance and excitement features of your customer's expectations is helpful in guiding how you act. Customers highly value friendly relationships yet relatively few organizations make a habit of that. There is a great opportunity to exceed customer expectations simply by being friendly.
At a personal level, everyone has "customers" in their day-to-day activities. Life is much more pleasant if you treat everyone as your customer. A warm, friendly smile goes a long way.

—Weimerskirch—

Minnesota nice misunderstood

THE STORY

An essential, moving part in a home control product was giving us trouble. Sometimes the supplier's batch of parts was perfect, our assembly went smoothly, and everyone was happy. But at other times, the supplier's parts were late, or marginally met specifications, and rework, rejections, and less-than-expected finished goods volumes afflicted the production line.

This pattern had developed gradually over a long time. As problems were shared with the supplier, remedial action and permanent process fixes were proposed by the supplier, but follow-through was inconsistent, and the situation persisted. It was either smooth, when parts met specifications, or the assembly line had to be shut down unexpectedly.

These were serious quality issues and threatened our ability to meet our customer orders.

Part of our newly established *Supplier Quality Improvement Process* (SQIP) worked on just these kinds of problems. We brought together our line personnel who touched a supplier's parts, product design engineers, and procurement people who dealt with the supplier on a regular basis. These SQIP teams were effective in resolving persistent problems using the philosophy of "lock the experts in a room together and they'll fix the problem."
We planned to do such an improvement with the supplier of an essential, moving part; the supplier that was persistently but intermittently causing our line shutdowns. We created our team of experts, the supplier identified theirs, and we made plans to fly

there and work together until the problem was solved.

Everything was arranged. We had statistics from receiving inspection, production, and our reliability analysis laboratory. They were collecting the same data. Once on-site, we'd investigate, study, analyze, make and verify improvements and leave when the improved process was reliably performing. It was an effective approach that had worked on many other supplier-related problems.

But after our team flew down to meet at the supplier's facility, we were greeted with a non-disclosure agreement (NDA) we each had to sign before being allowed to enter the facility. It was a one-way NDA; they were not agreeing to keep our data and analyses confidential. This NDA prevented the full team from discussing or observing process steps in the manufacture of the supplier's part or in our use of their part in our production. NDAs often cropped up because a supplier was making similar parts for a competitor.

WHAT WAS THE PROCESS OF DISCOVERY?

Past dealings with engineers, procurement, and production personnel and this supplier had shown a "Minnesota Nice" face when working through immediate issues. The "my way or the highway" confrontations were avoided, and people had worked around things that really should have been discussed, reviewed, and documented.

As leader of SQIP and this team, I refused to sign the one-way non-disclosure agreement. After uncomfortable discussion, I told them they had broken their promise about working together cooperatively. And, that we were leaving.

We left, flying home just a few hours after we had arrived. An expensive trip.

But the experience became lore with the division. Be nice, but facts are facts and if the suppliers wouldn't work with us to fix their product issues or help us fix our problems trying to use their products, then say a "nice" goodbye and find another course of action.

Minnesota nice

The stereotypical behavior of people from Minnesota to be courteous, reserved, and mild-mannered, is popularly known as *Minnesota nice*.

The cultural characteristics of "Minnesota nice" include polite friendliness, an aversion to open confrontation, a tendency toward understatement, a disinclination to make a direct fuss or stand out, apparent emotional restraint, and self-deprecation.

From Wikipedia, the free encyclopedia

The supplier was dropped for all division procurements as soon as qualified alternatives were found. Future sales calls to our division were rebuffed. The newly qualified vendor qualified their parts and our production processes using their parts had no line shutdowns.

LESSONS LEARNED:

"Minnesota Nice" was misunderstood. When communicating our production problems with their parts, the supplier interpreted the absence of aggressive and angry behavior on our part as weakness. Compared with other, angry customers we were pushovers in their mind.

The message learned from our "wasted trip" and shared throughout the division was a mandate that all suppliers **"Be honest with us and do what you promised. Or, we will find someone else who will."**

HOW YOU CAN DO IT TOO

Be gracious in people interactions but be clear and firm about facts and issues. Failures and non-conformance are data points. Treat them as facts that must be confronted. The facts are the things to discuss and agree upon.

Minnesota nice is fine for the people interactions, but the problems with process should be objectively stated and aggressively pursued toward resolution.

As in "I like you and your company, but your products are defective or deficient in these aspects, and if you cannot fix the process causing those problems, we must part ways."

—Fechter—

Promotion to action

THE STORY

Early in my career, I was monitoring a research and development project for high speed sorting systems to be used by the US Postal Service. One important test site was in New York City (NYC), near Madison Square Garden. Upon arrival at Pennsylvania Station, under Madison Square Garden, I walked a short bit to my hotel.

This was my first visit to NYC, and to a hotel whose name was well-known for decades. Upon nearing my room, I saw that each room was equipped with double, rounded doors, creating fat doors having little closets within. Guests could open their room-side door and hang items needing washing or dry cleaning within the curved door's closet space. Later, hotel staff would stop by, unlock and open their hallway-side door, pick up the laundry and deliver it later without anyone needing to enter the room itself. I thought it was *cool!* Excellent first impressions of this classic hotel.

It was late, so I unpacked a few things and went right to bed.

Whoops, one leg at the foot of the bed gave way and the bed slumped in that corner. I found something to prop up the bed and went to sleep.

Subway noise rattled intermittently from a sidewalk grating outside of the hotel and the noise woke me up in the middle of the night. I hadn't closed the drapes and saw that a full moon was suspended over the city. I didn't turn on the room lights because I wanted to see the moon overhead. My window was a bit foggy, so I wiped it with my hand to have a clearer view. Beautiful. First overnight stay in New York City and it was already special.

I went back to bed.

Later, upon waking to full sunshine streaming into the room, I saw that my pillow and the sheets were heavily streaked with black soot. I looked at the window where I had watched the full moon and realized that I hadn't been wiping away dew or room fog last night. Rather, the window had not been cleaned in ages and the "fog" I wiped aside in the moonlight was accumulated cigarette smoke and soot on the glass surface.

The bed's leg wasn't broken. It was missing. And from the pattern of visible wear on the several, thick telephone books I'd used to prop up the bed in the dark, they had obviously been used for that purpose many times before.

I took a shower, scrubbing my hands thoroughly to remove the fine soot. Then, reaching for a towel, I realized that the only cloth available in the bathroom was a washcloth by the sink. With that tiny "towel" I dried myself and then got dressed. I was prepared to tell my tale of woe to colleagues when we met for breakfast, but my tale was topped by a colleague also staying at the same hotel.

When he had taken a shower and reached for a towel, he found no towel, no washcloth, no floor mat... and he resorted to walking dripping wet from the shower to the bed and using his pillowcase as his towel.

Decades earlier the hotel had earned a reputation as a first-rate classic. By the time I visited, the reputation was fading fast. We didn't stay there on any future trips to New York City.

Why am I telling this story when the title of this article is *Promotion to Action*?

Well, it's a case in point. The hotel story is sad and funny. It caught your interest because it was a bit unusual. But it was **TMII** – *too much irrelevant information* if your interest is promotions and action.

TMII comes at us all day long.

An essential skill to managing is the ability to separate the information you need from a stream filled with irrelevant information. To filter out distracting or useless information, I need to ask, **"What do I need to know?"** to manage a process, to find defects, to minimize cycle time, etc. That's when data become useful.

Internet marketeers have developed ways to keep you attending to **TMII** and forget the job you started – think of Clickbait* sites.

---

*Clickbait— a form of false advertisement, uses hyperlink text or a thumbnail link that is designed to attract attention and to entice users to follow that link and read, view, or listen to the linked piece of online content, with a defining characteristic of being deceptive, typically sensationalized or misleading.

A "teaser" aims to exploit the "curiosity gap", providing just enough information to make readers of news websites curious, but not enough to satisfy their curiosity without clicking through to the linked content...

Long before the Internet, an unscrupulous marketing practice known as bait-and-switch used similar dishonest methods to hook customers. Like bait-and-switch, clickbait is a form of fraud.

https://en.wikipedia.org/wiki/Clickbait

While you may have enjoyed the hotel story, it took you from your primary task and took your time. We all need a reliable way to keep awareness of what we **need** to know, while blocking irrelevant material. **TMII** steals your day and your attention.

TMII starts young…

"Dad jokes" are funny but corny. Grandpa jokes are worse -- such preposterous tales and unreasonable claims that the grandkids are compelled to giggle and correct grandpa's assertions.

Some easy grandpa questions might be "What would happen if you weren't born on your birthday?" Depending on their ages, grandpa might see puzzled looks. But with time and maturity, those grandkids learn it's an impossible question and reply with giggles, "Well then that would be your birthday!"

Or, grandpa's preposterous claim that people only need to buy one book in their lifetime. What book? A dictionary. The words in story books, history books, technical books, and others are already in the dictionary so why not just pick and choose the words from the dictionary instead of reading the words someone else used to create the story? "Ohhh, grandpa!"

That's why we say, *"A dictionary does not a book make."* Someone's analysis, creativity, or experience is essential to find the correct words to efficiently tell the story.

WHAT WAS THE PROCESS OF DISCOVERY?

Here is how I learned some filtering basics so that I could have a steady stream of useful, actionable information and block **TMII**.

With my first promotion to an executive level, I didn't just move to an upper floor with a grand view. Yes, it was a grand view, but more promotions with finer views gave me less time to look because higher level positions were becoming more leveraged and more impactful, so I spent less time looking out the window and more time looking within the organization.

That grand view of the local environs is nice. However, the real fun after promotion to a management position is that you can see, understand, and impact more of the big picture – viewing and impacting things at the company-wide level rather than from a limited perspective within only a department.

You're no longer just an individual contributor or a supervisor of individual contributors. You're now an executive -- a manager of managers.

Not a passenger, you're now driving a key vehicle in the company caravan. Parts of the company are formally your responsibility to change and fix, to challenge how things are done, and then to take action to improve things. Meetings become course-changing navigation sessions where ideas become strategies and strategies are turned into budgets. Where needed resources like money, people, equipment, and workspaces are made available – so you can turn ideas into programs and projects that bring the strategies and tactics and goals to life.

This is heady stuff.

Then data start rolling in.

- *Some are spot on useful as received* – cashflow per project, or units shipped versus units ordered.
- Some shine light on previously unknown discrepancies, or opportunities disguised as problems.
- Not all data are things you want or need to know.
- Some aspects might impact processes for which you are clearly responsible. Other data also roll in about aspects that aren't your responsibility.
- They say that facts and figures scream for attention, but it isn't clear to whom some of these data are screaming or what particular kind of attention they seek.

For example, after one of my promotions I started receiving huge, paper printouts quarterly – inches thick (or for those who are digital natives rather than the paper printout generation, think of receiving an e-mail with a 5-gigabyte spreadsheet attached).

The printout had statistics about equal employment opportunity results. Ratios and percentages and categories and cross-tabulations of all types in the quarterly tomes.

The fat printouts were TMI – too much information. Actually, **TMII** -- *too much irrelevant information*. It was like receiving raw weather data about the speed of winds aloft over Canada, and information about the amount of precipitation falling in Oklahoma, snowpack depths in the Sierras, traffic delays in Casper, Wyoming, and dewpoints in Seattle. Volumes of data but most of it irrelevant if I'm focused only on the threat of frost to my orange grove in Florida.

Lots and lots of facts in the quarterly reports. But it was like a dictionary having many words but no author selecting which words (that is, which data) would tell me the story I needed to know about frost and my oranges. *As in the grandpa sidebar story, "a dictionary does not a book make."*

My company was tracking the number of women and men by job grade, by age, by years of experience, by region, and by year. And it tracked the number of Pacific Islanders versus Native Americans versus Asians and other groupings. And so on. It covered all US operations and tens of thousands of employees.

With the naïve enthusiasm and impetus to act -- that comes with being recently promoted and made privy to this kind of detailed reporting -- I scanned it and highlighted "interesting *TMII hotel* stories" and noted lots of **TMII** facts and jotted down many side notes.

They'd *"obviously"* sent me these reports because I could make a difference. But without the benefit of knowing the goals, and who owned which part of the results, I was very frustrated.

So, I finally sent one of my "noted and highlighted" printouts back to the head of Human Resources and asked, "What actions am I supposed to take after I receive this?"

Turns out that those quarterly reports had been initiated many years ago and went out automatically. Why did managers and executives at my level received these particular reports? Because managers at my level received these particular reports.

Repeat. Why did I receive the reports? Because managers and executives at my level received the reports.

The head of Human Resources heard my question and acted. The automatic distribution had started before his tenure. He stopped automatic distribution of the inches-thick quarterly reports to all managers.

In its place he started a process to update and communicate equal opportunity goals for the company as a whole and for its major divisions. People like me were then expected to look at the metrics for their division to compare actual statistics in our part against the company's equal opportunity goals. Which goals were our goals was clarified, but the skinny reports that followed no longer showed **all** equal opportunity employment data for **all** units in **all** locations. Just mine. **TMII** was blocked.

The question was no longer, "What actions am I supposed to take after I receive this?" Rather, with managers and executives now receiving shorter, focused reports came the responsibility to develop action plans to improve the way we did things -- in our part of the caravan -- to optimize equal opportunity by finding and utilizing diverse talent in our part of the firm.

Long ago, when data about equal opportunity metrics were unavailable, a major push had occurred to set up and communicate those missing metrics. It wasn't wrong at that time to share the entire data set, but it became unwieldy and unnecessary. It was **TMII** – too much irrelevant information.

LESSONS LEARNED:

What you measure is indeed what you manage. But before one starts measuring, or immediately after a first-ever baseline has been established, goals and their timeframe must be stated.

If the measures don't shine a light on opportunities to take action and improve outcomes, then why measure?

And, say out loud -- to be certain everyone knows and is in agreement:
- who owns which goals?
- does each goal describe by how much the status quo must be improved?
- and by when is each owner expected achieve those improvements?

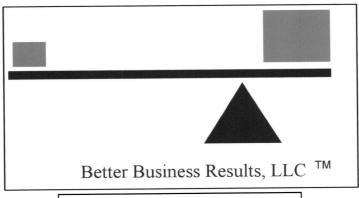

Better Business Results, LLC ™

I built the leverage concept into my **Better Business Results** consulting practice -- as illustrated by its logo

HOW YOU CAN DO IT TOO

- Ask. Why is something being measured? Who receives those measures, and what are they expected to do about them? What processes are making the numbers be where they are today? What will change them?
- Ask. What is the goal? And what measures will inform you that the goal has been met?

Knowing about winds aloft over Canada provides data. But are those the metrics *you* need?

Deep Work: Rules for Focused Success in a Distracted World, by Cal Newport, 2016

Deep Work uses memorable stories—from Carl Jung building a stone tower in the woods to focus his mind, to a social media pioneer buying a round-trip business class ticket to Tokyo to write a book free from distraction in the air. It delivers no-nonsense advice, like recommending that most serious professionals should quit social media and that everyone aiming to be creative should practice being bored.

First:

To figure out what you need, close your office door and tell everyone you're not to be disturbed.

Time for **Deep Work** →

Second:

Look at your list of goals – your department's and your personal goals.

Then, read and answer the questions in Category 4.1a (below) of the Baldrige Performance Excellence Framework.

Your answers will ensure that your operations reviews will cover measures and data and gaps that warrant your action and that will filter out time wasters like the funny, sad stories about my New York City hotel – no more **TMII**.

4 Measurement, Analysis, and Knowledge Management (90 pts.)

The **Measurement, ANALYSIS, and Knowledge Management** category asks HOW your organization selects, gathers, analyzes, manages, and improves its data, information, and KNOWLEDGE ASSETS; HOW it uses review findings to improve its PERFORMANCE; and HOW it learns.

4.1 Measurement, Analysis, and Improvement of Organizational Performance: How do you measure, analyze, and then improve organizational performance? (45 pts.)

a. PERFORMANCE Measurement

(1) **PERFORMANCE MEASURES** **How do you track data and information on daily operations and overall organizational PERFORMANCE?** How do you

- select, collect, align, and integrate data and information to use in tracking daily operations and overall organizational PERFORMANCE; and

- track progress on achieving STRATEGIC OBJECTIVES and ACTION PLANS?

What are your KEY organizational PERFORMANCE MEASURES, including KEY short- and longer-term financial MEASURES? How frequently do you track these MEASURES?

(2) **Comparative Data** **How do you select comparative data and information to support fact-based decision making?**

(3) **Measurement Agility** **How do you ensure that your PERFORMANCE measurement system can respond to rapid or unexpected organizational or external changes and provide timely data?**

From: https://www.nist.gov/baldrige/publications/baldrige-excellence-framework/businessnonprofit

—Fechter—

Servant leadership

THE STORY

I was sitting in my office at work one day when my boss walked in. He had just come from his own boss's staff meeting where it was reported that the "Big Tester" was down and that had stopped the production line. The "Big Tester" was a complex electronic test system that was critical to the production process. It had been designed, built and was maintained by one of the departments I managed. My boss said, "Getting that thing up and running again has to be your top priority for the day."

So, I went to my manager who had responsibility for that tester. I told him that his priority for the day was to get the tester up and running again. He came back in just a few minutes and said the tester was up and running. I said "Oh, great. You have it running already." He said "No, the tester was never down. It has been working fine all the way in through here."

I went back to my boss to report that the tester was up and running and that it had never been down. I asked who had reported that it was not functioning. He said it was the Director of Production. I tracked the story down and finally discovered that it was the Production Foreman who had reported that the tester was down. I called him and asked him why he had made a report that was not true. He said "I never said it was malfunctioning. I said it was down. My operator did not show up for work yesterday, so it was down." He got by with it. Nobody suspected him of any responsibility for the production line going down.

Did he lie? Technically no but effectively, yes. I wondered why he would report misleading information. Apparently, he was afraid of what would happen to him if he told the truth. I went back to tell this to my boss, but he was not interested. He had done his job. The tester was up and running and that was the end of it as far as he was concerned.

This scenario describes a classical business environment. It is a command and control style with information flowing up the organization and commands flowing down the organization. Information often gets distorted on its way up the organization as it did in this case. As a result, commands coming back down are frequently faulty.

WHAT WAS THE PROCESS OF DISCOVERY?

With the advent of the quality movement in the 1980's, the classical command and control management style was gradually replaced with a concept called servant leadership. Two concepts are involved in servant leadership: GEMBA and the 5 Whys.

GEMBA, a concept originated in Japan, means "the real place." It is where the work is done, and the value is created. Under this concept, organization charts are drawn upside down from the traditional model where management is on top. It is diagramed with supervision and management below the operator. Supervision and management are there to support the operators in performing their jobs. Each successive level of supervision and management has an increasingly broader view of the overall system and can solve more and more complex problems.

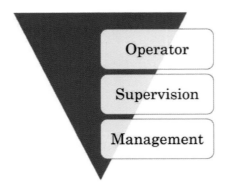

The "5 WHYS" also originated in Japan. It consists of a series of "why" questions. It is an iterative process. Each successive question is based on the answer to the previous question. Usually, by asking the question "why" 5 times, the root cause of the problem will be discovered. The root cause problem can then be solved, and the problem is permanently removed.

LESSONS LEARNED:

A great deal of information is lost as communications travel up and down the chain of command. People are afraid that they will be blamed for problems and will be reprimanded. As a result, they often bend the truth. The concept of servant leadership puts management in the position of solving problems rather than punishing employees.

Servant leadership employs the concepts of GEMBA and the 5 WHYS. Under the command and control management system, root cause problems are never solved. They recur over and over again causing wasted time and resources. Under servant leadership, problems are permanently solved saving time and money.

In the case of the "Big Tester", the servant leader would have been present on the scene and would have wanted to get at the root cause of the problem. They would have known that the problem was that the operator did not show up for work. They would not have had to rely on faulty information. They could then have gone to work to determine if there was a system problem and could have fixed it.

In the case of the "Big Tester", they would have asked questions like:

1. Why would the Production Foreman feel it necessary to lie?
2. Why did the operator fail to show up for work?
3. Why is operator absence a chronic problem?
4. Why did the operator not report that he or she would not be at work?
5. Why was there no back-up plan to replace the operator?

The late quality guru, W. Edwards Deming, always said that 85% of production errors were the result of system problems not operator errors. When production problems occur, supervisors and then managers are present on the scene to analyze the problems and then permanently fix them. The production line stays down until the problem is solved. Usually, this happens very quickly since everyone is present and is knowledgeable of the situation. This system leads to continual improvement in the processes.

HOW YOU CAN DO IT TOO

If you are in a supervisory position, you can employ GEMBA and the 5 WHYS. They apply to any job or situation.

If you are an operator, you can effectively employ the 5 WHYS. Consider any problems you have in accomplishing your job. Ask the 5 WHYS. Why does the problem occur and what is the root cause? You can then recommend actions that can be taken to remove that root cause and make your job more enjoyable.

Value creation

THE STORY

DEFINING WORLDCLASS

In the time of my career, business journals always portrayed Honeywell as a good but not great company. The common view was that we had enormous potential in the markets we served but, somehow, we were never able to realize that potential. We were not able to execute our strategies as well as we should have. We were operationally challenged. As Corporate Vice President of Quality, I felt it was my job to help Honeywell realize its potential. To do that, I had to work hard at getting people to be systems thinkers. I wanted them to understand the system by which a company creates value for all of its stakeholders.

I made it a point to travel around the Honeywell Corporation a lot to see what we were really like. Whenever I went into a plant, I would find something that I thought was a world-class performance. Not the whole operation, but a given practice. I remember being at one management meeting where I said "I am convinced that you could take any management practice and somewhere in the Honeywell world we employ that practice as well as any company in the world. So, what we need to do is be more uniform in that and employ those world class practices in every business unit around the world, consistently."

During those years, I reported to a brilliant man who had a very short attention span. Everything he did, he did very quickly. Anything you communicated to him, you had to do quickly. I was trying to show him what Honeywell should and could be. I decided it would be easier to communicate with him if I used as few words as possible. I challenged myself to describe a world-class company on one sheet of paper. My intent was to give people a vision of what Honeywell could be. Here, on one page, is my characterization of a world-class company.

> **Worldclass Characteristics**
>
> - Aggressive, visionary leadership with breakthrough expectations
> - Shared destiny, loyalty-based customer relations
> - Flat, horizontal organizations with talented, energized employees
> - Fast, streamlined processes delivering customer value
> - Comprehensive performance benchmarks
> - Superior financial performance relative to peers
> - Sustained growth driven by innovation and strategy execution
> - Corporate citizenship as a competitive advantage

WHAT WAS THE PROCESS OF DISCOVERY?

But visualizing a world-class company does not mean realizing a world-class company. To energize Honeywell to become world-class, I needed a focused strategy and a comprehensive plan to execute that strategy. Without that, we would be much like the Cheshire cat in Alice in Wonderland

Cheshire cat in *Alice in Wonderland*

If you don't know where you are going, then any road will get you there.

Source: commons.wikimedia.org

My strategy was to create a vision of "what" we want to happen. In my article on MAKING THINGS HAPPEN, I stated that a system contains all the necessary components and those components are all in the proper relationship with each other. In that article, I included a diagram of a management system to show "how" to make things happen. I still wanted to create a diagram to show "what" we want to happen. We needed to find the road to world-class.

However, before I could teach other people to be systems thinkers, I had to learn how to do it myself. The development of a VALUE CREATION MODEL was an evolutionary endeavor. My first attempt was rather internally focused. It really dealt only with the processes within the organization. A colleague looked at my early model and said, "Where is the customer in this?" An obvious oversight, so I added the customer to my model. Shortly after that, I was making a presentation to Honeywell's Board of Directors. One of the directors said, "I don't see people in your model." Another obvious oversight. Finally, when I learned about the European and Japanese emphasis on how companies impact society, I added that in.

LESSONS LEARNED:

Organizations exist to create value for all of their stakeholders. There is a complementary relationship among stakeholders – the more value the organization creates for one stakeholder the more value it creates for all stakeholders. Organizations that create outstanding stakeholder value share a common set of world-class characteristics.

Ultimately, I developed my VALUE CREATION MODEL as shown below.

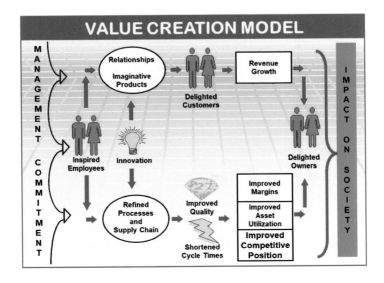

The model simply says that it takes bold leadership to inspire employees. Those inspired employees create innovative products and services and form loyalty-based relationships with customers. That delights the customers who reward the company by buying more resulting in revenue growth. That delights the owners. Inspired employees also innovate to refine all physical and managerial process within the company and the entire supply chain. That results in improved quality and shortened cycle times. That in turn, improves margins, asset utilization and competitive position. That too delights the owners. But the great companies have a higher purpose than serving their immediate stakeholders. Their purpose is to have a positive impact on society and make the world a better place to live.

Every great company is led by a person who has what I call "breakthrough expectations." Not impossible expectations, but expectations that push the organization to the limit of its capabilities. That results in the organization achieving far more that anyone thought possible.

World-class organizations have a deep understanding of their customers and their customers' requirements and expectations. They provide value to their customers and their customers are loyal to them. That value is delivered to customers through streamlined processes performed by employees who are talented, inspired, and engaged in the work they perform and the objectives of the organization.

World-class organizations also deliver superior financial results relative to peers. They do this by setting comprehensive performance benchmarks so that they know the performance levels they must achieve. They then set aggressive goals and put measures in place to make sure they are achieving their goals. They achieve these goals of sustained growth by executing innovative strategies.

World-class companies always have a higher purpose than just making a profit. They want to have an impact on society and make the world a better place to live.
Every successful organization has these common characteristics. Unsuccessful organizations fail in their own unique way.

HOW YOU CAN DO IT TOO

I have discovered that many people from different organizations have found these words and diagram to be helpful in their work. Hopefully, they portray a picture of how an organization creates value and can achieve world-class performance.

—Weimerskirch—

You actually read those memos?

NOTE:
This story originated in the days of paper
communications – memos, letters, reports. But the
moral of the story and its recommended tactics apply
equally well to today's predominantly electronic
communications.

Perhaps it is even more meaningful in the era of
electronic communications because the planning and
thought required to create paper documents of old is
often overlooked or incompletely done in quick texts or
e-mails.

THE STORY

Each week, the Engineering Department managers – about eight of us – would gather for an update meeting. It was in the days of paper memos. As we each arrived, we'd say "Hello" and then put a copy of our weekly update memo in front of each chair around the table on our way to the chair we'd occupy for the meeting.

The agenda was informal and collegial. We heard first from the director of engineering about company news and updates from the division leaders, then his summary of *hot button* items, project progress reports, business volume forecasts, and recent sales numbers.

After discussion and some Q & A about specific items, we'd each give a mini version of the same topics, specific to our functional areas. We covered things like product development, process engineering, tooling updates, personnel updates, and scheduling issues.

As managers went through their area's news, we'd occasionally write personal notes about things they were reviewing, things that touched our function or any action items that needed our follow-through. At the end of the meetings we'd disperse, bringing the paper summaries handed out at the start of the session.

I had only been working in "industry" for about six months. Prior to that I had only worked in academia and federal government agencies. A few days after receiving those handout memos at the update meeting, I was walking down the hall with John. I asked him about a potential production issue he'd noted in his weekly. He stopped in his tracks. He looked truly surprised. His immediate response (I'd been on the staff for only about six months) was, "You actually read those memos? **Really!?**"

I was surprised that he was surprised. He was highly regarded throughout the division, he made sure things got done per his promises, and he was an extraordinarily likeable colleague.

I wondered... Were those update memos intended to be informative or were they shared weekly just as a perfunctory exercise? Everything was new to me in my first industrial setting. I had curiosity to learn everything I could – including reading the weekly memos from each manager. He had been there for years, had many direct reports, and had much experience with the other staff members.

As time went on and my experience increased, the weekly meeting handout memos continued, and many more memos arrived throughout the week from project managers, salespeople, manufacturing, and elsewhere. I tried to read them all, but I started feeling swamped. Maybe this was why he had been so surprised that I not only *read* his weekly memo but that I *had a follow-up question* about its contents?

WHAT WAS THE PROCESS OF DISCOVERY?

It takes a while to get over the novelty of a new job environment, before one sees how the process works and understands cases where it doesn't work.

I started keeping mental notes about how much time and effort was required to read the written communications from staff and engineers and technicians, and from company management. It wasn't just the time needed to read the communications, but also the time required to appropriately act on the memo contents.

That was a weak spot. Many memos and reports were encyclopedic in length and detail, but too few had any closure of actions recommended or needed.

I am an efficient reader, but it always took more time and careful re-reading to ferret out what I should do after I had received the memos. This wasn't because I was new to the firm; it was because something was missing.

Just by chance I noticed a magazine advertisement from a paper manufacturer. To this day I'd like to thank them, but too many years have passed to remember the name of the paper company. Their ad's message was that communications were not effective *unless the recipient knew what to do or not do after receiving the message.* Memos needed to be explicit about what ACTION was expected of recipients.

ACTION -- that was the missing ingredient. Engineers and managers were almost obsessive about including every detail, every metric, every issue, and every topic they judged relevant to a memo or report's contents. The paper communications were voluminous.

But they didn't have what we would term today "a call to action."

Being a newcomer to the company, I didn't yet know that it was beyond my pay grade to initiate policy. But, with enthusiasm I drafted a new policy for all written communications within the division. It was quickly approved, published, and in use throughout the division.

The policy prescribed:

1. **Every memo must have an ACTION section. And only people on the "To" list could be expected to take action.** Those on the "cc" and "bcc" list could NOT be assigned an action. If any of the people on the cc or bcc list were supposed to do something, they must be moved from cc or bcc to the "To" list.

2. Most memos should have a **SUMMARY** section, no more than about a page. That SUMMARY should set the context for the ACTION.

3. The memo creator always had the option to add an unlimited amount of information in a **BACKGROUND** section. Writers were informed that the policy required that recipients must read only the ACTION and half-page SUMMARY sections but were not required or expected to read the background section. It was optional.

Complaints started soon after the policy was put into practice. Engineers complained that the engineer's job was to supply the facts and the boss should be able to figure out what action was needed; some thought it unfair to ask the memo creator to request or recommend specific actions.

Some people waited a very long time for follow-through and then understood that their memo had gone to a "cc" person who was not expected to take any specific action. Only those on the "To" list could be requested to take action.

Over time, people saw the positive impact of writing clearly described, measurable action items. Stated clearly, those action items could be debated objectively because everyone was looking at the same action, not trying to figure out what the author really wanted, if they had failed to be specific about the action.

FYI was an accepted action, **if** it meant that the memo was only *For Your Information*, like an update but not something that required readers to do anything after reading the message.

LESSONS LEARNED:

It was not perfect. But memos became shorter. Detailed engineering notes were written in the permanent engineering notebooks, but not in the background or summary sections. People discussed, prioritized, argued about, and resolved action items because now they were clearly stated.

HOW YOU CAN DO IT TOO

You put a lot of professional thought and analysis into a topic before you write a message for others. Be mindful. What ACTION do you want people to Start doing, Stop doing, or Keep doing after reading the memo?

Name names. Use active voice, "I recommend" not "It is recommended." Include enough information in the summary to describe why action is needed, the "return on investment" if actions are taken, and who should do what by when.

It is normal to have a high level of back and forth communications as people develop ideas and projects. That's normal discussion. However, if you are consistently doing communications rework – contacting the memo writers to figure out what actions they seek, it is time to invoke the **Summary, Action, Background** approach.

—Fechter—

You just shut down production

THE STORY

Imagine that you are an automobile manufacturer –

> I need your cost center number; you just shut down production

Ford, or Toyota, or Reo, or Chevrolet, or… and you sold one of your car lines to another auto manufacturer. Maybe you sold your Super Rally Reo Star line to Chevrolet.

You created a highly integrated style – putting the Super Rally Reo Star icon design into the dashboard with thousands of tiny Super Rally Reo Star icons subtly embossed onto the dashboard surface, and sewed into the seat fabric, and molded into the steering wheel, and so on.

Your supply chain procurement professionals have been hard at work to ensure a steady pipeline of parts intended for use in assembly of the vehicles. With the sale of the Super Rally Reo Star line to Chevrolet you have a dilemma – for how long can Chevrolet continue using Super Rally Reo Star parts after Chevrolet purchases the product line?

Customers are aware of the sale and know that during the transition some cars sold by Chevrolet will have Super Rally Reo Star logos all over the interior and exterior of the vehicles. This kind of situation is not common, so manufacturing personnel have little experience in the best way to transition and what the ideal timetable should be.

That was the situation in the late 1980s when *Honeywell Information Systems* sold a majority of its computer business to *Compagnie des Machines Bull* and *NEC Corporation*. It was a cooperative transition with the three parties, and a beginning example of how "big iron" computer companies were merging and reinventing themselves to supply not just machines, but also services, software, and systems integration with equipment made by other providers.

Our facility had been focused on building mid-sized computer systems; its large systems were manufactured in another US facility.

As time moved forward, Compagnie des Machines Bull (France), Honeywell Information Systems (USA), and NEC (Japan) changed the name to Honeywell Bull, and later to Bull HN.

During the transition from Honeywell Information Systems to Honeywell Bull, there was "reasonable flexibility" but no rigid dates to change the company name on printed materials and instruction manuals, technical reference documents, and the exterior "skin" of the mid-sized and large computers. Eventually, the pressure increased to complete all name changes on the equipment. It was time to make a hard change to use the new company name exclusively on everything and no longer sell product or distribute printed documents labeled Honeywell Information Systems.

In 1977 I bought a new Oldsmobile Delta 88 automobile, with the famous Oldsmobile Rocket 88 V-8 engine.

Except it wasn't an Oldsmobile Rocket 88.

In 1981, a federal jury decision forced General Motors to pay $550 each to over 10,000 purchasers of 1977 Oldsmobiles that contained Chevrolet engines, where the consumers believed from Oldsmobile advertisements that they were buying a new car with an Oldsmobile Rocket 88 V-8 engine.

General Motors argued in court that the practice of changing engine parts had gone on at General Motors for "many years." Their perspective was that the name on the auto referred to the GM division stood behind the product, not who made all the parts.

GM lost the argument. The jury concluded that Oldsmobile advertising implied everything in the car was from Oldsmobile, not from some other part of General Motors.

The issue kept coming up in operations meeting at all levels. But no department or function had the formal responsibility to make the change dates firm. It was unstated, but I believe that managers were reluctant to have their budgets absorb the cost of scrapping perfectly good parts from inventory that were identical in every way with new parts and documents, except the name.
The controversy persisted. So, I stepped in.

I called a meeting of senior executives in marketing, manufacturing, sales, and distribution. We reviewed what needed to be done. After a long, long meeting and after hearing from everyone, we reached a consensus of the need for a firm transition date. But the actual date was still unstated.

At that time, I announced that as of a specific date -- about six months in the future -- no product with the old name would be shipped. Only product with the name Honeywell Bull.

We went around the room to verify that everyone supported the decision. There were no dissenting voices. Smiles, and a clear date. I documented the decision in a paper memo to participants and others. "As of 01 January, no more panels or parts labeled *Honeywell Information Systems* or *HIS* would be used, only Honeywell Bull."

Summer melted into fall, and then Thanksgiving and then Christmas season.
Then, in the first week of January, I received a call from the local head of manufacturing. They were shutting down production and needed my cost center to charge the costs of overtime and supplies because "my" dictate made them shut down production.

Why? Because no one had translated the months-ago decision into orders for new panels with the new names. Instead, they just kept using the old ones until 31 December. Then, the no-ship rule came into effect, and manufacturing shut down.

We made urgent adjustments, allowing continued use of remaining old-style panels only after orders for new-style panels had been signed-off. Customers were not affected. My cost center did not have to pay the expenses.

WHAT WAS THE PROCESS OF DISCOVERY?

Initially, it was rewarding to take charge with cooperative colleagues to resolve a unique, confusing, never-before-experienced problem. That is, to fix a messy problem not of our own making but impacting our business lives.

When it blew up with the production shutdown in January, we acted quickly to do what hadn't completely happened at the first meeting. This time, **Who** will do **What** by **When** was articulated.

LESSONS LEARNED:

1. Absent specific authorization, if no one else is assigned the responsibility, circumstances can yield responsibility and authority to whomever steps up to the plate... especially if there is controversy.
2. The HOW was left unstated. Who will do what by when? What consequences will show us that the intended and agreed-upon actions actually happened? Left undefined, actions were expected from those attending the meeting, but knowing what to do is not the same as actually doing it. People left the meeting knowing about the many steps required but without any names assigned, required actions lapsed.

HOW YOU CAN DO IT TOO

Problems will happen. After the dust has cleared and the symptoms and bad consequences have been addressed it's time for a public or private postmortem.
What was the $Y=f(x)$ process you actually used? Was it planned or *ad hoc*? Record the emotion of what happened. Where did the process fail?

ACT on what you learned from the Five Whys.

Ask the five whys:

Example: Your vehicle will not start. (the problem)

1.Why? - The battery is dead. (First why)

2.Why? - The alternator is not functioning. (Second why)

3.Why? - The alternator belt has broken. (Third why)

4.Why? - The alternator belt was well beyond its useful service life and not replaced. (Fourth why)

5.Why? - The vehicle was not maintained according to the recommended service schedule. (Fifth why, a root cause)

From https://en.wikipedia.org/wiki/5_Whys

We all learned the five whys as children:

For want of a nail the shoe was lost.
For want of a shoe the horse was lost.
For want of a horse the rider was lost.
For want of a rider the message was lost.
For want of a message the battle was lost.
For want of a battle the kingdom was lost.
And all for the want of a horseshoe nail.

"For Want of a Nail" is a proverb, having numerous variations over several centuries, reminding that seemingly unimportant acts or omissions can have grave and unforeseen consequences.
https://en.wikipedia.org/wiki/For_Want_of_a_Nail

—Fechter—

Chapter 10
Results, not hopes

📖 Customer satisfaction

THE STORY

Shortly after I returned from a trip to Europe, I got a call from the airline. They were taking a survey to see how satisfied I was with my flight. They were interested in the outbound leg only, not the return flight.

The woman started asking me a series of questions and asked me to rate my satisfaction on a scale of 1 to 5 with 5 being very satisfied. Question number 4 was how I enjoyed the wine served on the flight. I explained that I didn't drink any wine on that flight. I explained that I make it a practice to not drink wine on the outbound leg of an international flight because it dehydrates me, and I don't feel very well when I get to my destination. (I have since changed my practice).

The woman continued on with the remainder of the questions. After she had checked all the boxes, she asked "Now Mr. Weimerskirch, is there anything else we could have done to make your flight more enjoyable?" I replied, "I'm not sure what you could do about it, but I noticed that about half of the passengers wanted to sleep on the flight while the other half wanted to talk. Could you do anything to help people sleep if they wanted to while the other people talk?" I could tell that she ignored my comment since there was not a box to check for that information.

At the end she said "Now let's come back to the wine. How did you enjoy the wine on the flight?" Realizing that she had to check all the boxes, I replied "The wine was great. I really enjoyed it."

> There is another story about customer satisfaction surveys at a manufacturing company. Management was putting a lot of pressure on the Customer Service Department to have a high level of customer satisfaction. There were consequences if the numbers didn't look good. As a result, the numbers did look good but that didn't seem to correlate with the number of customer complaints they were getting. As management dug into the details, they discovered that the survey team was discarding information from customers who were dissatisfied or very dissatisfied. Their reasoning was that those customers were not objective and therefore should not be counted in the database.

WHAT WAS THE PROCESS OF DISCOVERY?

These stories illustrate that one must be very careful about how data is used.

First of all, the woman taking the survey was not trained in why she was taking the data. She was just recording some numbers so that she filled out the form. She was not aware that her objective was to collect some valuable information that could be used to make improvements in the airline's service. I'm sure she was able to report back that she had gained a lot of valuable information from that customer satisfaction survey. In reality, she had collected false information and she ignored the only piece of valuable information I had given her.

Secondly, there is a tendency to want the data to look good. We do not like unfavorable feedback even though that is most helpful in making improvements. One must be careful how you interpret data.

LESSONS LEARNED:

What you measure is what you manage. The most fundamental reason to collect data and measure something is to improve. It is important to get information not just data. Setting numerical goals can be detrimental if employees don't understand the purpose of the measurement.

Numbers can be deceiving. Most customer surveys use a scale of 1 to 5 with 5 being very satisfied. Yet, many people never give a 5 rating because they believe 5 is perfect and nothing is perfect. Other people give all 5's unless they can think of some specific thing that could have been done better. It is necessary to look for little innuendoes in the data being reported. Keep in mind the fundamental premise that the purpose of measurement is to improve. Constructive criticism is the most helpful information in making improvements. Be careful how you interpret data. Be sure you are getting information not just data.

Some of the best information is not quantitative at all, but rather subjective or narrative. For example, the woman taking the airline survey might have noted the reason why I did not drink wine on the outbound leg of a flight. Do other people feel that way too or was I just an outlier? The information might have helped determine what type of beverages to serve on an airplane.

Some studies show that customers usually don't complain when they are dissatisfied. They believe a bad company wouldn't take any action anyway.

Instead, they simply tell 13 other people about their bad experience. In reality, customer complaints are some of the most valuable information available. If customers take the trouble to complain, they usually present opportunities to improve customer service.

HOW YOU CAN DO IT TOO

In this age of the internet, it seems that virtually every customer transaction results in a customer survey. If you are on the responding end of a survey, try to give valuable information. Pay less attention to the numbers and make a comment if you have ideas for how service could be improved.

If you are on the receiving end of a survey, pay close attention to how you interpret the data. Try to get qualitative information that gives you ideas on how you can improve. And if you are evaluated based on numerical survey data, make sure it is fair and objective.

—Weimerskirch—

I got flamed

THE STORY

I learned a lot.

As part of the first company-wide quality improvement efforts I initiated, we trained several thousand people across the USA about what quality means, how quality can save or sink a company, and how important it is that each person understand and act on that knowledge -- as if their job depends on it – because it does.

After individual contributors, operators, support staff, managers, supervisors, and division executives attended week-long Quality Colleges, supervisors and directors were charged with launching projects to make improvements. Many projects were set up; I was able to grease the wheels by providing funds from my project cost center.

Projects reported on their weekly meetings with people from all three shifts and from most physical locations. Lots of smiles. After a reasonable time, I wanted to see what kind of results were being delivered, so I asked for copies of project reports. No project had yet closed.

This team reported that it met weekly and had received suggestions from operators, support staff, and engineering. That team reported that it used the last hour of the Monday shift to share suggestions with the entire department, so that those in the department who were not yet on a team would know what was happening.

And so on...

With very few exceptions, the reports I received noted no product quality improvements, no ergonomic improvements to reduce injuries, no schedule improvements, no cycle time improvements, no cost reductions, no defect reductions, and no customer satisfaction improvements.

I was extremely disappointed that so many dollars and hours had been spent by the many quality improvement teams, but we had very limited, tangible improvements to show for it.

So, I changed the rules for anyone who wanted to continue using the cost center or start a new project. I made it a policy that if the charter of the project didn't include an objective definition and measurement of the criteria for sunsetting the project, then funding ceased or wouldn't be approved.

The response was immediate. In the next days I "met" many, many supervisors and directors in person who worked in the million square foot factory building. And I received angry telephone calls from offsite locations with the same complaints – "Why are you shutting down all the quality improvement teams?"

I got flamed!

Managers and supervisors complained that FINALLY the company was asking people to think about quality in all jobs, but I was shutting down those teams. People wanted to keep meeting to voice their complaints.

I learned that for most managers and supervisors the meeting itself was the objective – the lively discussion about quality, the camaraderie, the things that would improve if only quality improved, the ways that things could be better, etc.

Unfortunately, our Quality College had had an **unspoken** assumption that people would take action once they understood quality.

For three reasons, the assumption that people would act -- once they understood quality and its importance -- was a false assumption:

> 1) while the presence of defects or rework was known and understood to be bad, people working IN the process lacked the authority or resources to change whatever in the process was causing the problems,

> 2) unless the solution was obvious, we'd provided no tools to discover non-obvious causes, and

> 3) necessary actions seldom had an owner's name attached to inform everyone who had the responsibility to make proposed changes happen.

The biggest and most impactful error on my part was failure to require that each proposed project have a measurable endpoint stated. Something like:

> "This project will improve
>   (*improve what?* -- *State it*)
>   by (*How much?* -- *State it*)
>   by this date (*When?* -- *State it*)."

WHAT WAS THE PROCESS OF DISCOVERY?

I had developed fact-based lists of Costs of non-Quality – defect rates, missed ship dates, customer complaints, rework, and more. But post-Quality-College teams were mostly established independent of those lists – without specific targets related to

Costs of non-Quality. Once I asked for reports of tangible improvements, it became obvious that the current roster of improvement projects was not going to achieve the desired results.

LESSONS LEARNED:

Any proposed project should be treated like a small business loan from a bank.

Applying for your business loan:
- the context (the current process) should be described
- the business opportunity **specifically** described (defect reductions, cycle time improvements, or similar)
- exactly **what will be better – and by how much** -- if the project is funded and undertaken

And just like a bank loan, **no funding is available unless**
- the business model can be explained
- the list of needed resources includes how much of what, why it's needed, and when it's needed
- the measurable changes expected, **how you will know,** and by when.

HOW YOU CAN DO IT TOO

Ask the right questions. You needn't be a subject matter expert (SME) – the SME is the group asking for resources to do the improvement project.

They need to translate the things of the project into an investment opportunity.

Ask the Page 33 questions (see box on next page).

How I acted on what the flaming experience taught me -- Page 33

When subsequently launching a company-wide quality improvement effort at a nation-wide firm with over 30,000 employees, I mandated that no project could start until the form on *Page 33* was completed and approved.

Page 33 put into practice what I'd learned after getting flamed during my earlier experience.

- **Area for Improvement**: (e.g. Improved customer satisfaction, better communications as measured by, or less waste)
- **Goal:** Describe what will be different at the conclusion of the project. List the **specific** things that will be different, and **how different** they will be.
- **Measurement:** How will you measure what is different? Do you have a baseline measure before the project starts?
- **Benefits:** Describe the impact the changes will have, and how you will measure the impact. Describe impacts of the completed project:
  - as seen by customers
  - as seen by associates within the company
  - as seen by shareholders
  - as seen by the community

—Fechter—

📖 Eureka -- puzzle solved

Musings on a rainy Sunday morning at the lake

THE STORY

When our family first saw Neuschwanstein Castle in Bavaria we were agog for hours as we toured its many rooms.

Walking back to our rental car, our teenage son said that visiting Neuschwanstein had long been his dream, but something he thought would never happen.

Source: Wikimedia.commons

His Neuschwanstein memory was renewed when he gave us a 2000-piece puzzle -- a painting of Neuschwanstein. The puzzle is huge. We have finished parts of it and can recognize the castle, but there are many details yet to be completed. In the context of puzzle-solving I had my "Eureka!"

Profound "having intellectual depth and insight". Or, a more exciting way to say it, *Eureka!*

The ancient Greek scholar Archimedes reportedly proclaimed **"Eureka! Eureka!"** after he had stepped into a bath and noticed that the water level rose, whereupon he suddenly understood that the volume of water displaced must be equal to the volume of the part of his body he had submerged. ... He then realized that the volume of irregular objects could be measured with precision, a previously intractable problem. He is said to have been so eager to share his discovery that he leapt out of his bathtub and ran naked through the streets of Syracuse.
https://en.wikipedia.org/wiki/Eureka_(word)

---

moment. It was a rainy afternoon at the lake; I'd just spent several days immersed in evaluating applications for the Minnesota Quality Award. It's synonymous with the Malcolm Baldrige Performance Excellence award.

Taking pause, I sat back, watched the rain and the ducks and geese outside and then returned to the applications.

The Baldrige model diagnoses how well an organization is doing on criteria proven to deliver success. The application document guides organizations to describe how systems, processes, and measurement systems deliver results.

Examiners for the Minnesota Quality Award use a tool called the Expected Results Matrix (ERM). Here is how it works.

It's like a search engine looking through the full document. Every time a goal, a wish, a hope, an expectation, or similar is described – **anywhere** in the application document – it is added to a list of expected results.

Usually, this full list of expected results is bigger and different than the specific goals listed in the Results category or the strategic and operational plan. And in that way, the ERM helps discover whether there is a way to deliver "everything" the organization aspires to achieve.

The application's questions and answers paint a picture of big targets, but not all the other wishes, hopes, and expectations -- those many other things that are part of the whole picture. When you have a picture of the whole picture – the finished puzzle -- solving it becomes far, far easier. Similar colors go together, everything fits together as a system, and it's obvious when a piece is missing.

Sounds complicated, but it isn't. What you have is a picture of what the puzzle should look like when all the pieces are present, all in the right position.

Just as the Neuschwanstein puzzle with its 2000 pieces looks complicated, it is actually a big picture that is made up of many small things.

Photo by John Fechter

The tool for painting a picture of your puzzle comes in three parts:
1. the large, major goals an organization aspires to,
2. the many antecedent goals that are essential to enabling each major goal,
3. a collection of little systems for each subordinate or little goal, *each with its unique measurement and a feedback loop.*

Once done, you can see the picture of the finished puzzle:
- the combination of an expected results -- the big and little
- a table showing each subordinate system/process (Input → Process → Results) that collectively will achieve the big and little results

- and a table showing essential measures of things within each system/process to ensure it is working properly

The Expected Results Matrix is a fuller picture of the puzzle -- what the organization expects, wants, or needs to become real.

> Despite the fact that customer needs can become very numerous, each requires a means of measurement, a goal, a product, and a process design.   Dr. Joseph Juran

---

Strengths and Opportunities for Improvement (OFI)

When assessing goodness or issues with processes, a standard approach is to group similar "Strengths" together and similar "OFIs" together.
Strengths are those areas you do well and want to *keep* and build upon.
Opportunities for Improvement (OFIs) are areas that need to be improved by changing the Xs – by *starting* or *stopping* something.

$$Y=f(x)$$

WHAT WAS THE PROCESS OF DISCOVERY?

My Eureka was to realize that two simple additions will guide companies to solve the puzzle. Using the full list from the Expected Results Matrix, they need only to

> 1) define the processes/systems necessary to deliver each of the goals, the wishes, the hopes, the expectations and then
> 2) define the critical measures for each of those many processes/systems.

That done, the organization has a roadmap of actions to put into place any missing processes/ systems for each of the goals, the wishes, the hopes, the expectations.

> As noted by Steven Covey, "Begin with the end in mind." Starting with a picture of the finished puzzle does that.

In my simple, $Y=f(x)$ world, the ERM (Expected Results Matrix) is like a search engine sniffing its way through the application document. When it sniffs out a stated goal, or a gap, or an expectation, or a result, or an $f(x)$ ingredient, it copies that to an ERM. And with the Expected Results Matrix format one can later tag each item with **who** is charged or responsible to do **what** by **when**.

LESSONS LEARNED:

- The ERM should be expanded to include every goal, wish, hope, expectation, or similar. And for each item in the Expected **Results** Matrix, the Expected **Process** Matrix should describe how that goal will happen. And for every process and every step, the measures needed – Expected **Measurements** Matrix.

The secret?
In engineering-speak, it's a system, $Y=f(x)$.
Results (Y) are a function of causes (X's).

In everyday terms, it's a cause → effect model.
To quote Arnie Weimerskirch, former judge for the award, "Baldrige represents the leading edge of **validated management practices** that produce superior business results."

$$Y=f(x)$$

- Using an ERM and then creating the roster of needed processes and associated metrics for each item in the ERM gives non-prescriptive but clear guidance on what to **start, stop, or keep** for every Opportunity for Improvement (OFI) that finds its way into a feedback report.

HOW YOU CAN DO IT TOO

Use active reading, active listening. When reviewing, reading, or hearing a project proposal, or a strategic plan, or any plan describing something wanted but not yet a fact, use active reading or listening.

That is, from the start to finish as you learn about the plan, make a note whenever you see something that's not on the "Big Picture list" but is stated indirectly or implied or assumed. If you don't see that detail, then ask.

Neuschwanstein is the castle. But it cannot exist in the air. It needs to be grounded on the mountain, there are trees in the surrounding area, there is blue sky and some clouds.

When the Big Picture is painted, capture the surrounding detail. Only then will you have a picture of the finished puzzle so you can subsequently identify those many expected results that are crucial to enabling the Big Picture to actually build the castle.

Such detail is not visible if you are only shown the castle in isolation. If the presentation – orally, on paper, in a document or whatever -- does not show the many little things, then a first task is to charter people to add those details so you can see the castle in context, not in isolation.

Doing this you can use your painting tool and its three parts:

- the large, major goals an organization aspires to (The castle)
- the many antecedent goals that are essential to enabling each major goal (The mountain, the trees, the sky, the clouds)
- a collection of little systems for each subordinate or little goal, *each with its unique measurement and a feedback loop (These are the many, many little things that collectively enable the Big Picture).*

—Fechter—

Rich and Famous

THE STORY

A colleague working with me on a company-wide improvement project related an experience he once had when communicating a similar plan within his company.

> What Do You
> Want **Me** to Do?

On the day of his program launch, he assembled a *town hall meeting* of all personnel.

The setting was a big warehouse area. Everyone was there – executives, line workers, design engineers, clerical support staff, and many other functions. With sincerity and enthusiasm, he spoke about the value of quality, about doing the right thing, and about enjoying a work life without rework – where the causes of errors and defects had been systematically found and weeded out.

Immediate action was sorely needed at the firm.

They had many quality issues. His was a project no one could refuse because the benefits were so urgently needed.

- Customers would benefit from the renewed focus on quality.
- Employees would be satisfied that all their work counted and none of it was wasted effort.
- Production costs would be lowered because rework would not be needed.
- And market share would soon rise as people outside the company started to see how things were improving.

He was extremely satisfied with the smiles and long applause at the conclusion of his presentation. People were much enthused to hear about the company-wide plans. It looked like a perfect start to better days.

Then, while leaving the town hall session, he met a long serving, seasoned, maintenance man. That person too was smiling and shook Steve's hand. "Steve, that was one of the best presentations I have ever heard."

And Steve smiled back. But before he could add his own comment or say *Thanks*, the maintenance man added this question, "So, what is it that you want *me* to do?"

At that moment, Steve said he realized that something was missing – in a major way. While the presentation had painted a dire picture of how very much the project was needed and had painted a glowing picture of how much better things would be AFTER the project was done, something was missing. His presentation had not included *how* those changes would happen or *who* would do *what* or by *when*.

Missing from the picture was an answer to "So, what is it that you want *me* to do?"

It was like asking someone just starting out in life, "*What is your ambition?*"

And hearing their reply, "*I want to be Rich and Famous.*"

But rich is undefined, and famous is undefined. Rich in money terms? Rich in friends? Rich in health? And famous for what? For novels written? For starting a company from scratch? For discovering a cure for a dread disease? Without defining the end goal, and how it would be measured, the path to becoming rich and famous is vague. And the chance of achieving the undefined goals is very thin.

WHAT WAS THE PROCESS OF DISCOVERY?

Working at a nationwide bank on a company-wide improvement effort I once faced the same question. What do you mean by *Rich* and what do you mean by *Famous*? What are the specific goals, who are the stakeholders, and how will all stakeholders know we're reaching those goals?

Banking has obvious financial metrics, lots of rules, regulations, and compliance mandates.

Traditional measures of success were basic and looked at WHAT but seldom looked at HOW and often included only a subset of stakeholders.
But the bankers picked up the challenge to answer –
what did they mean by *Rich* and what did they mean by *Famous.*

We needed specifics so they and everyone else could answer, "So, what is it that you want *me* to do?"

To clarify fuzzy or undefined targets, we held offsite sessions, weekend sessions, and on-the-job sessions to argue and agree about how to define our Rich and Famous, and then HOW to get there.

Our customers defined the primary goal – to be America's first choice ← **Are we there yet? How would we know?**

The *mission* is the business we are in. And the *values* are how good we aspire to be in achieving that mission

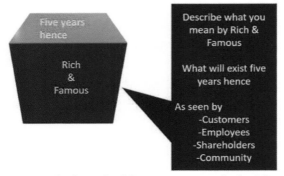

Customers and shareholders were stakeholders, with employees, and the community. All stakeholders have their own expectations. We state the mission and values and then we ask the stakeholders ← **Are we there yet? How would we know?**

That's the easy part...
For example, if a company value is an unwavering commitment to quality, what does that mean to customers, to shareholders, to employees, and to the community? ← **Are we there yet? How would we know?**

Here are examples of how the banking executives answered the questions.

Customer	All departments regularly ask and measure *what **their** customers have told them* matters the most.
Employee	100% of people employed in a department more than three months can identify their primary internal or external customer and can describe the three most important things those customers expect.
Shareholder	Costs due to poor quality (i.e., inspection, time, and personnel doing error correction, rework, and activities that don't add value to the customers) are reduced 10% each year.
Community	90% of full-time personnel participate in Habitat for Humanity projects annually

The hard part is to cascade this approach throughout the organization. In my unit, does the wording of a customer expectation *as-stated* fit as my unit's goal? Or does the wording need some tailoring to fit our unit, perhaps create a unique, substitute goal? Maybe we need to add a goal – derived from the stated customer expectations as a unique goal for our unit?

Next, we look at the value's wording seen through the lens of shareholder expectations; then through the lens of employee expectations; and then through the lens of community expectations.

With all that work done, we have also defined the measures we can use to answer the questions ← **Are we there yet? How do we know?**

Measure today's baseline before you start any change.

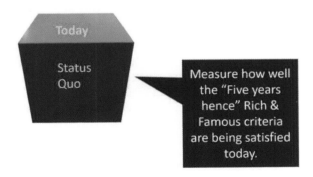

Unless you take actions, tomorrow will look just like today. That's simply because stating a goal is only the first step.

Action will make the goal become a fact, not just a wish or a hope.

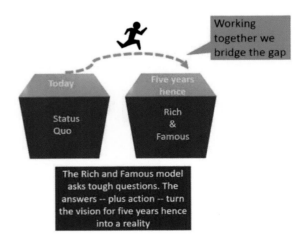

LESSONS LEARNED:

Customers, shareholders, employees, and the community are all stakeholders. All stakeholders have their own expectations.

We state the mission and values and then we ask the stakeholders ← **Are we there yet? How would we know?**

To become Rich and Famous, we need specific, measurable goals so we can find gaps.

Then prioritize which gaps are most important to close. Then develop a plan to close the gap and provide people and resources to make it happen.

Then, act, because without action, the status quo repeats endlessly.

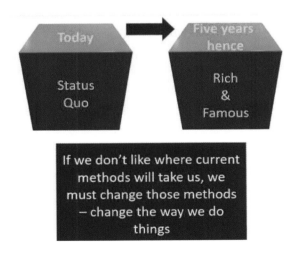

```
Goals → Measurements
  → Measurements → Gaps Identified
    → Gaps Identified → Projects
      → Projects → Resource Request
        → Resource Request → Resources Provided
          → Resources Provided → Team goals and actions
            → Team projects → Individual goals and actions
              → Results
```

HOW YOU CAN DO IT TOO

Personal Action Plan
1. My role in the value-added chain is to provide these products or services...
2. To these kinds of customers...
3. These indicators show my customers if improvements are happening...
4. The most important improvements my customers have asked for...
5. Actions I can take myself to deliver requested improvements to my customers...
6. Actions I cannot complete by myself and I need help from others...

—Fechter—

Use data to make decisions

THE STORY

On one of my trips to Japan, I was impressed with how they use data to make decisions based on fact.

We were staying in a 20-story hotel that had four elevators. We were there for a week. As I started to use the elevators, I noticed that a car was always waiting on the floor where I needed it. I thought, "How did they know I was coming?" This happened repeatedly. My curiosity got the better of me. So, I asked the concierge how they were able to do that. He explained that the elevators were programed to come to a stop on the floor where they were likely to be needed next.

In the olden days, elevators always returned to the ground floor when no one was using them. In later years, elevators stayed on the floor they were last used. In this hotel, they kept automated records of how many people were staying on each floor. Then they recorded how often the elevators were used by each floor. From this, they could statistically predict where the elevators would most likely be used next. Their system sure shortened the wait time for an elevator.

On this same trip, we visited a restaurant that made extensive use of data.

Their objective was to minimize food wastage while still making sure their customers were satisfied that they had had enough to eat. They recorded data like the following:

-How much food is returned uneaten?
-How much more do men eat than women and in turn, children?

-How much more do people eat for dinner than they do for lunch?
-How do people's eating habits vary with the time of the day they eat lunch or dinner?
-How do people's eating habits vary depending upon the day of the week?

We had a very good meal at that restaurant and had all we wanted to eat. We didn't waste much. They adjusted their portions according to the amount that each person would likely eat. The restaurant manager stated that their use of data in this way kept customers satisfied and improved profitability at the same time. The reduced waste also helped save the environment.

WHAT WAS THE PROCESS OF DISCOVERY?

This experience was the first time I had seen data used in these creative ways to make intelligent decisions. Obviously, in my jobs, I had made extensive use of data but here it was used at detailed levels by all employees on a day-to-day basis. It was so ingrained in their operations that it was not costly to do. It was simply what they did.

As I thought about it, I realized that this was an example of what is called "evidenced based management." Too often, we are inclined to speculate on what we think is true and then act on that. Usually the actual facts are something different and so our actions don't get the desired results.

LESSONS LEARNED:

It is important to use data (evidence) to make decisions. This is known as evidenced based management. Evidenced based management is a matter of determining the desired result and then identifying the data (evidence) that needs to be collected to determine the facts. By analyzing this data, actions can be taken to achieve the desired result.

HOW YOU CAN DO IT TOO

Collecting data is not difficult but it does take some discipline. Modern technology makes it much easier to collect data. For example, your iPhone will automatically record the miles you have walked in a day and the number of steps you have taken. If you want to lead a healthy lifestyle, you can set your goal and then walk the number of steps necessary to meet that goal.

—Weimerskirch—

What's the secret formula?

THE STORY

Oh! So that's how it works!

Shhh… It's a secret!
1. $Y = f(x)$
2. ROI
3. SSK
4. $K + A = R$

A giant *thank you* and many apologies to my two, older sisters.

When I was about 10 years old, they were recipients of some fantastic gifts – a tiny oven that could bake one cookie at a time, dolls whose eyes closed when you tilted the doll back, wind-up toys that raced and bumped and flashed their lights, and more. We had many happy times playing together with their toys.

But that's not what my thanks are for.

My giant thanks are for their infinite patience when I was still a youngster and used tools like screwdrivers and pliers to figure out how things worked.

> In the early 1950s, many metal, Japanese toys were made from metal food cans that had been recycled. That is, pressed into the shape of the toy. If you took the toy apart you could still see the Japanese letters and pictures from when your toy car was originally a tuna fish can.

I took apart the oven to figure out what made the light turn on and how it heated the baking space. I pushed the dolls' eyes back to look inside the dolls' insides to see what triggered the eyes to close. And I undid the metal flanges on wind-up toys to pull them apart, expose their innards, and figure out how the spring was tightened and how it drove the toys' movements.

My many apologies are for the condition the toys were in after my "investigations." In most cases the toys were returned in working condition but showing a lot of wear and tear. And some didn't work quite like they had when my sisters had first received them – but I never pushed either sister for a thank you when I returned their reworked toy in one hand and *also gave them some "extra" parts in the other hand.*

My reputation for taking things apart and rebuilding them spread; I found out years later that my youngest sister, when she was about age 10, yelled out, "Johnny broke the TV!" when the channel knob stopped working – even though I had been away at college for many months and couldn't have touched the TV.

WHAT WAS THE PROCESS OF DISCOVERY?

My curiosity to understand how things work continues to this day. And fortunately, I've learned how to learn without breaking the things that I'm investigating.

The things I've investigated, and watched, and studied have some strong similarities. Instead of toy ovens and wind-up toys, I've been blessed to understand and improve processes – companies' strategic planning processes, their manufacturing processes, health care delivery processes, hiring processes, R&D processes...What they all have in common is that they are all systems, processes, whether designed to be so, or it just happened.

Common to all processes, is, in engineer speak, $Y=f(x)$.

We use Y to stand for results. And the formula says that Y – the results – are a function of X. $Y=f(x)$. What's X? X can be anything that helps us get the results we seek, or anything that stands in our way and prevents us from getting the results we seek. We want to bake chocolate chip cookies. A great cookie is our Y.

And the Xs are the ingredients and the steps. We need chocolate chips. Flour, Water. Sugar. Those are things we need. But we also need an oven heated to the correct temperature. And we need to have the cookies baking for a specific duration in the hot oven. So, a great cookie depends on flour, time, temperature, chocolate...

The eyes of my sisters' dolls moved when I tilted the doll.

Y=closed eyes.

Changing from open eyes to closed eyes depends on:

- the length of the metal wire to which the eyes were attached,
- and on the counterweight inside the doll's head,
- and on having enough space that the counterweight can move within the doll.

Now let's look at the complex processes in our lives. Suppose that accidents and injuries are happening regularly on a nearby road.

The accidents are the Y. Accidents shouldn't be happening, but they are happening, regularly. What are the Xs? Are the accidents happening every day? At the same times? In all temperatures? Experts studied those potential Xs and concluded that most of our nearby road's accidents are happening within 30-minutes of closing time at local bars. That suggests what Xs need to change to lower the accident rate.

LESSONS LEARNED:

1. $Y=f(x)$ Cause and effect. That's the first of three secrets. Not too exciting to say it, $Y=f(x)$. But **extraordinarily powerful** if you look at any process through that filter.
2. The second is to look at the Y – today's results – and conclude that things are just fine, or that there is an opportunity to improve the Y. Improve by either getting better results from the process or improve by removing bad things that degrade our results. Look at that opportunity and calculate an ROI – Return on Investment. It doesn't need to be only money. For example, if

present processes see 12 lawsuits filed per month, the ROI could be expressed as 50% fewer lawsuits per month. If that ROI is valuable enough to you, then look at the third secret.

3. What's the third secret? SSK

Stay with me. The present process is causing a dozen lawsuits per month. What Xs, that is what causes are present or missing from our $Y=f(x)$?

No interlocks on the product so users are getting shocked? Users standing on metal ladders in water and getting shocked? To reduce the number of monthly lawsuits, we need to know what we must START doing in the process (for example, add an interlock to shut off power if the cover is opened).

What must we STOP doing (relying exclusively on labels and instructions advising to use only in dry environments?)

And what do we need to KEEP? (Requiring that users have a switch to energize the device rather than simply plugging it in.)

The Soviet visitor's factory tour

An old joke circulating in the 1960s tells of a Soviet visitor who wants to learn the secrets of capitalism and productivity. He visits an American factory and gets a tour of the entire operation.

He notices that when the factory whistle blows, workers walk inside and start working. When the whistle blows again, they walk out to eat their lunch.

When the whistle blows again, they re-enter the factory and resume working.

At the end of the day his tour guides ask him what he has learned about capitalism and productivity. He thanks them for sharing the secret.

"I now understand how to get people to work. We need to buy whistles for all of our factories."

Perhaps he didn't truly understand?

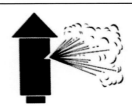

HOW YOU CAN DO IT TOO

First secret, identifying the Y, the result you want or don't want from your process. Don't start any improvement action if you cannot articulate the Y and can explain how you measure it.

Second secret, figure out the ROI, the benefit you'll see if the Y improves. Can you explain the ROI in objective, measurable terms? Don't start any improvement actions unless the ROI proves its worth to you. Its worth is either better results or the reducing known problems, so you no longer experience them. If the ROI isn't valuable enough, then you probably should look at other opportunities before you attack this one.

Third secret, analyze what the Xs are and how they impact one another to produce the Y.

Each domino has an impact on the others.

If the dominoes are not lined up properly, you will not get the desired end-result you seek – the Y

Then, take action to START things that aren't happening now, STOP things that shouldn't be happening, while KEEPING Xs that are already in the process and should stay.

Maybe a fourth secret? Have a bias for action.

Knowledge doesn't make things improve. And Knowledge plus more Knowledge doesn't make things improve. What's needed is ACTION. Knowledge + Action = Results.

$$K+K=K$$
$$K+A=R$$

It's a process.
  $Y=f(x)$.
     Results (Y) depend on knowing what to do and taking SSK actions.

TLA stands for *Three Letter Acronym*. Hearing TLA for the first time, people usually do one of two things, sometimes both.
   Response #1 = a groan and rolling of eyes, and then a smile because they have heard the TLA before. Response #2 = an "Oh!" and then a smile because they hadn't heard it before.

These TLAs can be **extraordinarily powerful**
   1. $Y=f(x)$
   2. ROI
   3. SSK
   4. K+A=R

—Fechter—

Live
Long
and
Prosper

Photo by John Fechter

This Vulcan salutation is a hand gesture
popularized by the 1960s television series Star Trek.
It consists of a raised hand with the palm forward
and the thumb extended, while the fingers are
parted between the middle and ring finger.

It was devised by Leonard Nimoy, who portrayed
the half-Vulcan character Mr. Spock on the original
Star Trek television series. A 1968 New York Times
interview described the gesture as a "double-
fingered version of Churchill's victory sign".
From https://en.wikipedia.org/wiki/Vulcan_salute